AF480206

MAKING LIFE RESPOND BY INNER WORK (Vol-3 of 3)

UNLOCKED : 100 SECRET LIFE-TRUTHS

Your Life Guide: Quantum Pathways to Prosperity

N.M. Nageswari

Copyright © N.M. Nageswari 2024
All Rights Reserved.

ISBN
Paperback 979-8-89544-372-9
Hardcase 979-8-89544-373-6

This book has been published with all efforts taken to make the material error-free after the consent of the author. However, the author and the publisher do not assume and hereby disclaim any liability to any party for any loss, damage, or disruption caused by errors or omissions, whether such errors or omissions result from negligence, accident, or any other cause.

While every effort has been made to avoid any mistake or omission, this publication is being sold on the condition and understanding that neither the author nor the publishers or printers would be liable in any manner to any person by reason of any mistake or omission in this publication or for any action taken or omitted to be taken or advice rendered or accepted on the basis of this work. For any defect in printing or binding the publishers will be liable only to replace the defective copy by another copy of this work then available.

Dedication

This book, born from the Presence and Grace of Sri Aurobindo, The Mother, and Sri Karmayogi, is dedicated at Their Feet.

Sri Karmayogi (Founder of the Mother's Service Society in Pondicherry) consecrated and surrendered his entire life to the teachings of Sri Aurobindo and The Mother. I offer my deepest gratitude to Sri Karmayogi, whose presence in my life has made the manifestation of this book possible for you to read today.

Acknowledgement

I am deeply indebted to the explorations of Mr. Garry Jacobs and Mr. Roy Posner, whose ongoing research into life and human evolution has enriched the concepts discussed in this book. Many of the life examples cited in this book are drawn from their research works. Their dedication and contributions in the field of human evolution and life response continue to illuminate Sri Karmayogi's legacy through real-life examples and profound insights.

Mr. Garry Jacobs is a key official in Mother's Service Society (MSS) for nearly 50 years and President and CEO of the World Academy of Art & Science. His inspiring and insightful daily video interactions regarding Life and Life response are available at https://karmayogi.net. The website links of their entire works are provided in the References section at the end of the book.

My heartfelt gratitude to Mr. Garry Jacobs, Mr. Roy Posner and The Mother Service Society for playing the role of GREAT AWAKENERS and for their continuous efforts in unravelling more of Sri Karmayogi's works and bringing transformation in the lives of people across the globe.

I extend my deepest gratitude to Mr. Garry Jacobs, for acting as a pillar for me and whose esteemed guidance, generous dedication of time, encouragement, and support proved invaluable in bringing this book to life. His unwavering inspiration has been a beacon of light in my life, for which words alone cannot express what my soul intends to.

I express my gratitude to all the teachers, visible and invisible, who have appeared in my life.

I extend my heartfelt thanks to Smt. Siri Khalsa and Sri Sat Khalsa, Spiritual Gurus of Excellence, Founders of Alpha Stars Academy of Excellence, Innermost Shift Coaches who groomed me as an Innermost Shift Coach and imparted me the knowledge of creating the inner shifts in others by inner work. This knowledge has helped me in giving birth to this book to awaken the excellence in you.

I am also grateful to my husband K. Rathinavel, and my friend A. Thiagarajan, for their enthusiastic support. Special thanks to my loving daughter, R.Shailaja who helped me in all possible ways to place this book in your hands.

Sincerely speaking, all being shared through this book has been received from the Divine and this grand Universe and is being offered back.

Preface

Have you ever felt a yearning for a deeper understanding of life's purpose? This book, "Moving Life from Within by Inner Work," offers an invitation to explore your inner potential and unlock a more fulfilling existence. The book content in the 3 volumes are based on Sri Karmayogi's writings.

Sri Karmayogi's writings were the outcome of his continuous Inner Work & Yoga through Consecration and Surrender and were based upon Sri Aurobindo and the Mother's revelations. Sri Karmayogi fondly called as 'Appa' had dedicated his life in making it intelligible and easy for people to understand the subtle laws of life, the significance of inner work, life response and to apply in one's day-to-day life.

'The kingfisher that returns with no food becomes the food for its young ones. Mother sacrificed Herself thus to us' said Sri Karmayogi. The Mother he refers to is The Mother of Sri Aurobindo Ashram, Pondicherry. What Sri Karmayogi said about the Mother's sacrifice is a kind of sacrifice he had also done for the humanity in silence and his outpourings through his numerous works spanning many decades on various subjects about Secret of Creation, Existence, Human Evolution, Human Life, Life Response, Inner Work, and Inner-Outer Correspondence, stands as a testament to his sacrifice.

Close to Sri Karmayogi's heart is Sri Aurobindo's book, magnum opus, The Life Divine. Life Divine book is Sri Aurobindo's principal philosophic work, a theory of spiritual evolution culminating in the transformation of man from a mental into a Supramental being and the advent of a divine life upon earth.

Life Divine is the most challenging book on Earth to read and comprehend because of the depths of the content and the massive language structure which Sri Aurobindo used in this book. Life Divine book contains all the answers to each possible question in this Creation.

Sri Karmayogi found the Life Divine book full of secrets of life-truths. He endeavored to make this book comprehensible to the people elucidating the principles of life truths, subtle laws of existence, and their practical applications through real-life examples. Throughout his life, he employed diverse methods to reveal these secrets, offering a broad pathway for massive opening to aspiring seekers.

Sri Karmayogi said that 'Sri Aurobindo's philosophy has earned the reputation of being incomprehensible. For over forty years I have been at pains to render it simpler.'

Sri Karmayogi had elucidated how individuals can achieve fulfillment in life by applying these profound truths, unraveling the complexities of human behavior, character, and personality through novels and literature. He authored two volumes in Tamil titled "My Family," where he elaborated on concepts of inner work, life, character, human personality, and behavior and life response based on the principles of Life Divine Book. Later, he additionally authored twelve volumes through a meticulous examination of the novel "Pride and Prejudice," delving into these concepts for each sentence in the narrative. He experimented with various approaches to simplify life's truths, making them accessible for practical application and enabling individuals to experiment with these principles in their own lives.

To read and fully comprehend Sri Karmayogi's extensive lifetime of work, one might need many lifetimes. Within the pages of *"Moving Life from within by Inner Work,"* I've distilled the essence of Sri Karmayogi's teachings on Inner Work that profoundly touched me. My sincere aspiration is that these insights will ignite lasting transformation and deeper understanding among readers.

There is greater meaning to our earthly life than what we think of. When we understand the true meaning of our existence, our life and evolution, life becomes immensely interesting. I hope this book of 3 volumes will awaken you to your buried inner potentials by raising your personality, understanding the true significance of life, quantum transform yourself by inner work, realise your inner true being and to accomplish vastly and lead a prosperous life. If the contents of this book resonate with you, I urge you to explore more on Sri Karmayogi's revelations.

Sri Aurobindo states, "A greater consciousness and life await humanity."

As sincere seeker in life, more is waiting for **YOU**. Your **TIME** is precious. Your **ENERGY** is precious. Your **LIFE** is precious. **YOU are Precious**. I invite you to embark on your Inner Adventure for Inner Work. Come; let us explore the **Marvel of Life!**

Table of Contents

Part V

SPIRITUAL

Seeing the Grace, Supergrace

Remembrance of the Divine and Spirit brings grace.

When we are not occupied by the past and are free from the burdens of the past, Grace accomplishes everything for us in our lives. Once grace is rationalised or explained away, it never returns. Gratitude and acknowledging the grace instead of self-justifying egoistically the grace, makes grace stay.

Karma and Grace

Non-acceptance of responsibilities attracts Karma. Acceptance of responsibilities attracts Grace.

The level of acceptance of responsibilities by us determines the level of acceptance of grace inside us and the acceptance of grace in our life.

Likewise the desire. Desire attracts Karma. Rather than fulfillment of desire, overcoming the desire gives greater fulfillment. Grace embraces us when we overcome the desire.

Grace removes the knots of Karma. If Grace comes by the front door, Karma goes by the back door. Grace brings spiritual revolution and evolution in us.

Our stabilised ignorance brings stabilised Karma. By embracing Grace, Karma dissolves. Lightning flashes in the sky without stabilising itself. Similarly, this fleeting Grace becomes stabilised when we choose to embrace knowledge and shed our ignorance. Like parrots in the cage we are in the cage of ignorance, karma and ego. Our stabilised knowledge brings stabilised grace.

Calling Grace

What we call comes. If we call Grace. Grace comes. Grace has power to break the cage of ego and has power to open a new world inside us. Our decision to transform ourselves is the determinant for the action of grace and to make the transformation happen. It is not the strength for transformation we require, it is the **strength for taking the decision to transform ourselves** which is required for the grace to act.

When Grace comes inside our inner being, our mind, heart, body opposes and revolts in all its strengths to the action of grace. It is the way of lower rejecting the higher. This is at the individual scale at the level of Jiva. One can imagine the magnitude the opposition which emerges against the grace at the world level, when the grace descends for the transformation of the world.

The level of acceptance of our difficulties is the determinant of the level of our acceptance of the incoming grace. The difficulties what we are experiencing currently in our life is the doorway for the future incoming grace to us. The change in our perception of difficulty to perception of grace, makes the grace act instantaneously.

Opposing the Ever-Present Grace

Man opposes grace and tells that Grace has left him. But the fact is inspite of negation grace never leaves man. Like air cannot leave us, gravity cannot leave us, even if we oppose. But man due to limitation in thoughts, create conditions and remain in the cage, preventing action of Grace. To make man conscious of his limitation, the same grace is required to make him understand that Grace has not left man but man has left grace.

Gratitude makes grace as supergrace.

More the crop grows, more the weed grows. When more knowledge comes inside us, more we become aware of our ignorance. We oppose with all our force and revolt against the workings of Divine grace in our lives. We are unable to recognise the grace as we act from our intellect and not from soul. Grace may not come into our life not necessarily in pleasant form but even in adverse forms and events. True wisdom lies in recognising the grace behind these difficult situations. In times of hardship, the Divine embraces us closely. Grace manifests in various forms—- good, bad, knowledge, ignorance. By setting expectations and fixing channels in our minds, we limit the action of the grace.

If one rejects availing scholarship in college, to continue education, fees have to be paid. Likewise, if Grace is rejected by us, we have to put efforts to attain the thing. As fees are required to continue the education, efforts are required to accomplish a thing which the grace has brought. Grace repeatedly comes unless we consciously reject. When an unimaginable responsibility comes on us and when we reject it, we are rejecting unimaginable luck in our life. Grace can bring luck and profit. For intellect to become graceful, our thoughts have to become silent.

Evolution teaches the entire creation, the joy of being. A wonderful grace carries us. Journey of humans is hard and long as they are in love with their bondage and fear losing themselves in light and freedom.

Man shifting his **faith in karma** to the **faith in the Divine**, invites Grace, which dissolves his past karma.

Human effort and Grace of Spirit

Human effort spreads horizontally when there is great energy but lacks the higher organisational capacity that is needed to rise. Capacity to organise at a higher level enables man to rise. In either scenario— horizontal expansion or vertical growth—only one movement is feasible, unless there is a continuous generation of greater energy from below. In that case, _man grows on both sides as a pyramid._

Spirit's Grace can be likened to an inverted pyramid spread all over the higher regions and trying to descend to man. Compared to what Spirit can achieve, what can be achieved by human effort is only a trickle and fraction. One is finite, the other, the infinite.

As the ascending human pyramid of effort intersects with the descending pyramid of Spirit's Grace, a complete sphere of divine action emerges. At this juncture, each point relates to every other point and maintains its relation of perfect integration, opening up infinite dimensions of action.

It is the chemistry of human effort of aspiration ascending to meet the grace of the spirit which brings instantaneous life response.

Conditions for the Grace

Grace represents the unconditional action of the Spirit, yet the impact of grace in our lives depend on our faith, aspiration, openness, receptivity, generosity and sincerity. The best possible response to Grace is Gratitude. Acknowledging that grace is unearned and expressing gratitude for it contrasts with feeling proud and justifying grace through egoistic arguments of deserving it.

It is mean to demand of others what we cannot do ourselves, while generosity lies in aiding others in what we are capable of accomplishing. **Karma, Compassion and Grace** are the **three life responses** to human consciousness. Karma is totally a response to our consciousness and actions. Compassion gives us more than we deserve. Grace gives unconditionally and irrespective of our condition. Nevertheless, the results of Grace still depend on us.

77

Intuition, Inner sense of Knowingness

When we live inwardly, it is possible to achieve a state of peace and inner equality that is untouched by the reactions of the outer nature. There is a knowledge deep within hidden. When we connect to our inner being and inner voice, we know the things from within. It is called inner sense of knowingness, intution.

What separates the outstanding from the rest of the people is, they remain strongly on their axis and rooted in bliss of their oceanic potential. They have a great sense of uniqueness, practice inclusiveness and connectedness, energy of love and inner knowingness. This requires the inner shift.

The secret of being outstanding is: "Seeking answers from within for what you love to do, love to have, love to know and be the unique expression of 'BEING' who you are."

As you work to architect, innovate and shape your future, there may be no reference and no one around you available to be referred. You may have to know things from within. There is no logic, no calculation, no profit, no loss. There is some intuitiveness.

When you look back on your lives, you may realise that many significant decisions, such as choosing your educational path, selecting a job, choosing a life partner, or deciding whether to undergo surgery during illness, you would have decided based on an intuitive understanding. When others ask you on what basis you have taken decision, you reply it as gut feeling or inner sense of knowingness. There was an inner voice, gut feelings inside which would have indicated you the course of action and you did it. It was less about logic and more about knowing and feelings of self-assurance.

When you love someone, you know that you love, and you know you love for sure and you know you are right. Maybe you can't explain it, but you do know you love from a place of Inner-Knowingness. Thus, there is a place of knowingness within & this can be sensed.

You get a 'sense of being right' beyond logics, **from** your **power Centre of Inner Knowingness** of being 'sure and right'. By growing aware of how you took decisions in the past by hearing your wise inner voice or accessing your Power Centre of Knowingness will greatly help you in future. You can learn the art of identifying your inner congruence signals and patterns. The truth about human potential is whatever we experience once, we can learn to do again and again.

You can walk into your memory lanes and see in the past, some such decisions you have taken from your inner knowingness and relive such moments. When you relive it, scan your body and see from which part of the body such sense has emerged. Many see it is from their gut, some say it is from their heart centre, some say it is from their head. You can see the pattern. If most of such decisions are emerging from the same centre for you, say heart, then your power centre of inner knowingness is heart. In the future, whenever you want to make some important decisions, you can focus on your centre of knowingness to know things from within. For many people the centre of inner knowingness may be the same every time when they make decisions but for others it may be different for different situations. One may experiment and see.

By becoming aware of your power centre, you can make right and wise decisions. It empowers you to find unique answers and work out unique ideas in your unique set of circumstances. You come to know what's right, and you become certain beyond logic.

KNOW-ingness brings NOW-ness

KNOW-ingness is to KNOW. In KNOWing there is NOW. One can't be in 'NOWness' without being in knowingness. To be in NOW, one has to KNOW.

Truly living in the NOW means we have to be AWARE.

- Wearing good and physically appearing good but unaware of bank balance.
- Lavishly spending on credit cards, your financial standing is standing on the loans and debts !
- Celebrating eating sweets and ice cream but not considering diabetes!!

This is not living in the present being fully unaware of your financial health or physical health. Living in the present means being present to everything there is in the moment and not being absent to everything there is in the moment. It is embracing the moment while being aware of the big picture. When you know your outer circumstances and map of your inner being, you make the best choices and the choices will make your NOW meaningful. The 4 Quadrant Decision making matrix which we saw earlier relating the Inner and Outer will be of great help in taking decisions by exercising the power of inner knowingness.

Scientific discoveries-Expression of Intuition

Scientific discoveries are not the result of experimentation, but of intuition. You can't uncover the formula for $E=mc^2$ by digging into any number of sand piles or performing numerous experiments. You discover that formula by opening your mind to a higher way of knowing. *Discovery is an act of consciousness,* not a lucky stroke of the shovel or pitch fork. The power to discover resides within the human mind and consciousness, not in the machine which is our instrument.

Inner sense of KNOWingness is INFINITE

When we give up the senses, our reason becomes intuition. The knowledge inside will never fail. Our Inner sense of Knowingness is infinite. It is the infinite consciousness. The Infinite consciousness within us enables us to see infinite opportunities everywhere. The finite consciousness sees difficulties. Mind's knowledge should become the soul's light. Our surface consciousness belongs to reason. Our deeper consciousness belongs to intuition. Reason justifies, intuition discovers, realisation confirms. The truth justified by reason is discovered by intuition and confirmed by realisation.

There was a devotee who took a deep interest in helping those who sought his guidance. Once a visitor came back several times and the devotee was eager to assist him. "Is there something specific you need?" the devotee asked. The visitor replied, "Every time I come to you, you speak exactly what I was going to ask before I even speak. You did the same today."

Spiritual faculties emerge when one takes to the Spiritual Force. The Spirit is invisible to our naked eyes. It rarely acts in the lives of ordinary men. When it acts, people see the results, not the Spirit, as we do not see the electricity that operates each piece of equipment we have. We see the fan running, the bulb burning, etc., but we do not see the electricity that operates them.

Inner Knowingness-Aspect of Spirit

Through consecration, one can awaken the inner Spirit and can bring it to the surface of one's lives, and can see the Spirit in action. It is felt as sandal fragrance, a sweet tune of music, a sudden sense of sweetness in the mouth, a live figure emerging from the picture of a God, etc. **Inner voice and inner knowingness is one such aspect and manifestation of the Spirit.**

When Spirit acts in life, we recognise the Spirit as luck, a fulfillment of our own unspoken desires deeply buried in us. By constantly aspiring and turning the gaze inward, one can connect with inner voice to empower oneself.

Connecting to your inner voice and developing your inner sense of knowingness helps you to make right decisions in your life courageously and to cheerfully move forward.

Shifting from Poverty to Prosperity Consciousness

Poverty consciousness struggles to accept Prosperity consciousness. It needs an inner effort out of self-choice.

Deep down, human perverted lower nature not allows Prosperity to enter even in one's life is the shocking truth. Man is capable of intolerant of Prosperity to himself unconsciously. It is the inner poverty in consciousness. It is the desire NOT to exert or intensely aspire.

Poverty is the desire **NOT** to see the **Prosperity** around.

Scarcity is the desire **NOT** to see the **Abundance** around.

Inner moves the outer. Outer is the reflection of the inner. Outer poverty is the reflection of inner poverty in being. Inner richness brings outer richness. We have to ascend from poverty consciousness to prosperity consciousness.

We have to ascend in the evolutionary plane at least in our thoughts. Our thoughts influence our DNA. Nerves remaining unaffected by sensations is the indication of dissolution of mind.

Life, business, work, family, fortune are expanding infinitely. Life is full of opportunities. We are unconscious. We have to move from unconsciousness to consciousness. In the measure one emerges out of ego, one can have a life of joy and abundance at home. Our entire life should shift from Form to Content. Rather than the Form, the visibility or appearance, the Content, the Substance of our consciousness, the makeup of our being -whether Poverty-Oriented or Prosperity-Oriented, whether embodying Victim mindset or Growth mindset, plays an important role and determines the course of life.

Character of Prosperity

In the political field, it is possible for a driver to become a Central Minister or a peon to rise to the position of a Cabinet Minister. We also frequently see an industrialist's car driver becoming wealthy or a VIP in his town. Some characteristics of Prosperity:

- Prosperity is neither ethical nor moral in itself.

- Prosperity moves to a mighty person who is ruthless.

- Prosperity is commonly found where there is organisation or power.

- It does not mean we need to accept Prosperity through whatever route it comes to us. We can choose only Positive Prosperity.

- Prosperity is not a true measure of success, particularly in a spiritually inclined country like India. There is no debate about the importance of prosperity. India's voice will not be heard in the world if she is a poor country. She will certainly be heard with more respect if she is wealthy rather than poor.

- Prosperity is not something to be avoided or shunned at all. Austerity is not simplicity.

- Domestic life does not seek austerity.

- It is evident that prosperity is a valid and rational goal for a householder.

- Prosperity reduces ignorance and illness.

- Prosperity inherently provides security.

- There is a direct correlation between prosperity and freedom.

- Prosperity comes to those who honor its necessary disciplines.

- The foundation of prosperity is built on organisation, common sense, industry, responsibility, honesty, and alertness in life.

- Desiring prosperity without fulfilling its basic requirements is mere wishful thinking.
- Prosperity is a better foundation of Spirituality than Poverty.
- Prosperity is organised energy, not determined by its ethical character.
- Prosperity is indispensable for health, education and happiness.
- Prosperity increases as we ascend the scale of human values: from the physical to the vital, from the vital to the mental, and finally from the mental to the spiritual.
- The greatest Prosperity issues out of Spirituality.

Spirituality is Prosperity

Prosperity of any kind is a form of spirituality. Spiritual Prosperity is everlasting, and never diminishes. Wealth by itself may destroy peace of mind; Spiritual Prosperity enhances mental peace. Spiritual Prosperity is harmonious. Prosperity enhances domestic peace. Prosperity increases overall discipline.

At a certain point, Prosperity begins to Self-multiply. No poor nation has ever led the world. No poor man has ever been heard or obeyed with respect. If any poor man leads, there will be a rich man behind him. India cannot become a global leader without her also becoming exceedingly wealthy. Wealth is the Truth of Life. Mother Earth delights in producing more and more; she doesn't like to be a barren, poverty-stricken Mother. The world will not unite around a poor nation with a primitive lifestyle. World unity requires abundance in our country.

Material prosperity and Spiritual prosperity: Welfare and Well-being

Spiritual prosperity brings an instinctive enjoyment to all things it encounters. Material prosperity arises from responsible, capable and organised work. Productivity is a hallmark of prosperity. Spiritual prosperity is an inner well-being that delights in its own existence and often seeks nothing from the outside. When engaging with the external world, it tries to give knowledge, energy, or even material help. Great souls are born with spiritual prosperity. **Welfare pertains to material life**, while **well-being belongs to the indwelling spirit**. When such a person visits a new place, it carries a prosperous vibration to that place. That person is expansive, cheerful, optimistic, and outgoing.

Pathways to Prosperity-Awake, Arise, Organise, Embrace Values

Whatever values we have accepted, is our universe. The divine and universe comes to us in our life as values. Whatever we accomplish in life, it is through our values. The universe touches man as values.

Prosperity stems from willingness to work for more. A person's potential earning capacity is the sum total of one's emotional equilibrium. Prosperity can be attained through several steps by seeking self employment, organising the work to express values, acquiring continuously higher skills. Awaking, arising and organising is the way to prosperity.

Process of shifting to Prosperity Consciousness

Shifting from Poverty consciousness to Prosperity consciousness will bring abundance in a person's life. By letting go of limitations and poverty consciousness and by embracing abundance mindset and prosperity consciousness, we can attract prosperity in life.

Poverty consciousness involves an inability to understand the means of progressing in life, focusing solely on limits, obstacles, and roadblocks. It reflects a lack of knowledge about the laws of success, which include:

- The power of aspiration to perceive possibilities and set goals
- The willingness to achieve those goals
- Cleanliness, orderliness, and personal organisation
- Positive attitudes towards others, life, and work

- The knowledge and skills to take one further
- The experience of success that energises and brings joy
- Not being bound by old, dead habits
- Overcoming the social barriers we perceive around us
- Avoiding blind adherence to rituals like slave
- A heightened sense of individuality rather than following the crowd and the herdal view
- Application of personal values one deeply subscribes to
- A willingness to make an all-out, persevering effort to succeed

Adopting these in our lives – as well as spiritual methods such as non-ego, soft speech, self-givng, inner silence, taking the other person's point of view, and consecration, etc will take us from poverty consciousness to great, even infinite-like success.

Daring to make the Switch and Inner Shift

From within, one can attract all that one wants to achieve, also known as The Secret, echoing the method of the Divine who created a universe from within Itself. The universe and entire creation is created and being sustained by the Supreme Divine from inside. Inner is moving the Outer. The real source, power, roots are within. The knowledge and practical applications of the "The Secret" by tens of thousands of people worldwide who have had astonishing, miraculous-like experiences along these lines is the proof of the INNER power of Attraction. We can bring about such results without moving a muscle; life simply responds to our focused aspirations by presenting opportunities. Thus, "the Inner Moves the outer." The same principle applies to shifting from a negative to a positive attitude. As soon as we make that switch, **positive circumstances appear at our doorstep from out of nowhere.**

This is the new perspective of life that is available to us. If you can grasp that – that one's aspiration and the spiritual force used in combination can instantaneously move life without any outer effort - you will see the infinite-like power that is at your disposal. This power is accessible to you right now and enables you to quickly evoke the infinite from the finite.

Seeing the Infinite in the Finite

How the Small Finite Opens the Portals of the Infinite-Interconnectedness of Events

The world is a web. We can say under our radar of tiny surface outward consciousness, there is an intricate infinite network where we can find each movement of our life is connected with others in this planet, each situation, each association of ours with other people. Sri Aurobindo says : "The stone lying inert upon the sands which is kicked away in an idle moment, has been producing its effect upon the hemispheres." There is immense significance in the insignificance. Many would have seen in their lives how one casual circumstance seemingly unimportant or one casual word or phrase has changed the course of life.

In any given moment, there are large and small acts related to a significant event. For instance, during a medical emergency, the focus may be on the patient and the rescue efforts, but there are also unnoticed actions, such as a supervisor arriving quietly, a nurse ordering medicine, and an elderly patient joking in his wheelchair. These various activities, whether directly related or seemingly unrelated, occur simultaneously. And yet in such circumstances, every and all events are in fact deeply interconnected, no matter how unimportant and distantly related they seem to be. Even the smallest, most trivial, or seemingly opposite action can influence the final outcome. To be sensitive to this process is to have a vision of life's true workings, which gives one the power to influence the world around us.

Significance of the Insignificance

In every situation in life, every element that presents itself serves a purpose. Even the smallest detail, including those that seem negative or opposed to our goals and intents, can be a means for its final resolution.. Therefore, we should not ignore or be irritated by anything, the smallest of the small can provide an opening to the infinite.

Then, if this is the case, then how can we become self-aware, all-aware? It all depends on our level of consciousness. To become more mindful of the various elements, movements, and activities in any given situation, it all comes down to our level of consciousness. An open mind and heightened sensitivity are needed to recognise the usefulness of each action in the context of the whole event. This awareness requires a still and silent mind, as well as a calm, steady, cheerful positive psychological disposition.

Sherlock Holmes Made Observation as a Science

Consider Sherlock Holmes. By employing keen, mindful, and multi-faceted perception, one can understand the importance of even the smallest action in the outcome of any situation, problem, or event. It was Sherlock Holmes who made observation a precise science. For observation to reach this level, it must be an act of sensing rather than mere seeing. Seeing or hearing is primarily a mental activity, whereas sensing enters into the object of observation and directly feels as it feels. Recognising the comprehensive whole, rather than just the obvious parts, is a spiritual quality known as "integral knowledge."

Perceiving this comprehensive whole, rather than just the obvious parts, is a spiritual quality known as "integral knowledge." Seeing the Infinite in the finite gives us Integral Knowledge.

The Marvel of Existence: Finding the Infinite in everyday life

Indian spiritual philosophy teaches that the infinite can emerge from anything, whether large or infinitesimally small. To the infinite Consciousness and Being, there is no difference between the two. Thus, the silly, the trivial and the negative and hostile also serve as instruments for progress and change. If we can learn to perceive this dynamic in our daily lives, then we will have a glimpse of the Marvel of existence.

Willingness to Make Small Corrections Opens Up the Universe

Swallowing one's ego and willingness to correct the slightest mistake suggested by another can open up an entire new world of possibilities. For example, in a partnership, one partner pointed out a minor error in the training materials for a workshop that the other partner had developed. The second partner felt offended that the first partner was emphasising a minor detail rather than considering the overall presentation. However, he suppressed his troubled feelings, refrained from voicing them, and went ahead and made the small change anyway. Suddenly a moment later for the first time the two were considering working together to market the entire 7-day workshop!

Thus we see that the small, even an apparent negative small, taken in the right light and right spirit can open the door to significant opportunities. The micro can be a gateway to the macro when embraced in the right way. Why is this so? The tiny and finite is great because it is interconnected with everything else. From the perspective of the highest consciousness, there is no distinction between the small and the large, the micro and the macro. Embracing the small instead of being hostile towards it can quickly lead to vast opportunities– and the universe will quickly open up.

Understanding the Divine Purpose in Evolution

Everything in the universe is designed by divine creative intelligence. Life of knowledge we term it as Divine. Life of Ignorance we term it as Undivine. Imperfections, suffering, and evil arise out of a life of ignorance. Egoistic life is a life of suffering and ignorance. Our ignorance, which is limited knowledge, is the cause of imperfections. We term something as un divine because we don't see the divine purpose behind each thing. Divine WILL can be seen in the meaningless actions of other people. The Divine unfolds itself in the evolution of Nature. To find the key of everything is the Divine purpose of our evolution. Suffering is due to the limitation of our consciousness. Limitation is in our egoistic consciousness. Limitation is only in the consciousness and not in the being. Imperfection, suffering, pain are a stage in our divine evolution. When we outgrow the need for pain, pain vanishes. Ignorance negates. Knowledge affirms. The ultimate evolutionary purpose of Divine is to find the Delight in Existence. Larger consciousness and life awaits man, says Sri Aurobindo.

Releasing the Infinite Through 'Complete Act'

According to Sri Karmayogi, any action, no matter how small—such as writing a check, cleaning a carpet, or having a meal—can instantly attract good or great fortune if executed to perfection. To perfect an action means transforming it into a "Complete Act," characterised by aspiration for achievement, inspired will, and persistent effort fueled by right skills, positive attitudes, and high personal values. Doing so will achieve our goal and much more, as the infinite will emerge from that finite, putting in our hands the same capacity as the Divine and Spirit.

This notion underscores the concept of Sri Aurobindo which he states in his Book-The Life Divine: Infinite can emerge from the finite. Every finite thing in creation has its source in a Divine Infinite. However it is hidden from us in life. And yet if we make any life activity a Complete Act, the infinite remerges and life responds out of all proportion.

Infinite Power of the Finite

To know the significance of the infinitesimal leads to the discovery of the power of the Infinite. Everything that appears finite, limited, ignorant, and powerless is essentially a frontal appearance of the Infinite. Behind each finite appearance lies an infinite potential. It means that every individual, every circumstance and every moment possesses infinite possibilities. It is then up to the individual to reach the infinite possibilities through consecration.

In addition to consecration, various methods can be employed to tap into these infinite possibilities. These methods include practicing higher levels of cleanliness and orderliness, avoiding wastage of resources, overcoming negative attitudes, practicing non-reaction towards others' intensities, refraining from blaming others, taking responsibility, making a decision overcoming ego and selfishness, feeling goodwill toward others, expressing gratitude, quieting the mind, exerting silent will, taking the other person's point of view, seeing negatives as an opportunities, greater harmony with others, and so forth. All these practices attract powerful positive responses, particularly when combined with consecration to the Spiritual Force. In essence, this combination effectively evokes the Infinite from the finite.

When you closely observe life, you'll notice small, seemingly insignificant circumstances around you that subtly mirror, reflect a significant event in the world occurring at that time. We often live confined behind our skin, preoccupied with our small personal affairs, not realising that at every moment the entire universe is inside and available to us.

> "Hold Infinity in the palm of your hand
>
> And Eternity in an hour."
>
> — (William Blake)

When we tune our inner to the Spirit and see the interconnectedness of everything as one stream, Infinity in terms of space, Eternity in terms of time, both can be overcome. Then one sees the instantaneous miraculousness and witness the Life Response phenomenon.

How can one begin to see the necessity and interrelation among all things in and beyond creation? Through constant consecration and constantly taking another's view, our minds expand significantly. This practice enables us to increasingly experience the utility and interconnection of all things, which gives us ultimate power of knowing, decision making, and action. This newfound awareness swiftly evokes the infinite from the finite in no time at all.

If behind every opinion there is a hidden opportunity and behind every attitude there is a hidden profit potential, then where were the limits to growth? The physical sciences regard infinity as a mathematical concept. We have not yet come to realise that in human life infinity is a practical concept. The potential for creation is truly infinite. Infinity really can be a practical reality in our lives.

Even through small acts, we have power to evoke infinity in our life.

Attention to a very small unknown Customer-Small Order Blossoms into Vast Orders Over Time

When an unknown customer from a neighboring state placed a $150 order with a flooring company, the sales manager of a flooring company decided to treat this tiny order by an unknown customer as if it had been placed by the biggest & most important customer the company ever had. Despite the order's small size and the customer's unfamiliarity, the manager opted to treat it with utmost importance, providing top-notch service akin to the company's largest clients. While the manager's actions didn't make sense to his staff, who saw the order's cost outweighing its profits, the manager persisted. But one thing led to another. The customer, delighted by the exceptional service, spoke to another company. This word-of-mouth recommendation resulted in substantial business for the flooring company, with orders exceeding $5 million over the next few years.

80

Shifting to Spirit,
Functioning from Spirit

Seeking other's spirit, following other's realisation is RELIGION.

Seeking one's own spirit is SPIRITUALITY.

Religion is following the awakened spirit of the other. Spirituality is awakening to one's inner spirit. Spirit is the substance of which the entire universe is made.

Consciousness + Object = Experience

Consciousness + Subject = Awareness

We have to expand our experience and raise our awareness of our experiences to go to the depths of our selves which is the subject. From consciousness of object we have to shift to the consciousness of the subject.

The throne of the king goes to his son. But doctor's son must qualify himself to be a doctor. He can't inherit from his father. Spirit can't be inherited. It has to be attained through aspiration through right choices in daily life. To invoke spirit all time is yoga. To invoke the spirit in a particular act is prayer. In fact invoking the spirit is more powerful than prayer because the spirit gives more than what we ask for. Spirit has the capacity of Alchemy. It transmits poverty to prosperity. It shrinks centuries to decades. Spirit means spirit of life, spirit of work, spirit of ideas, spirit of man. Invoking spirit we progress endlessly.

Man in life can't master life but man in Spirit can master life. Astrology is the mathematical formula of what life is. Invoking spirit is the formula to bring life response for what one desires to be.

Spirit lies beyond our character (swabhava) and centre of personality. As the personality rises to the occasion of unknown problems, calling spirit from there will solve any problem. Deeper the call, the more powerful it is. The strength of calm that descends upon one who calls the spirit, shows the depth of the call.

Invoking spirit activates the inactive capacities and ushers one to prosperity. All Prosperity is Spirituality. Spirituality is Prosperity. Tradition enjoins us worshipping the inner Brahman. The inner Brahman is the Spirit which is the flame residing in the heart's cave of the individual. It is an evolving soul. ***Spirit never fails; Man never fails to fail.*** The saying goes, man's outward victories are failures of the soul. The true and real victory is gain of evolutionary knowledge and growth of the consciousness which is the victory for the soul.

Awaking the deeply buried spirit may be the ultimate discipline. When one rests in the Spirit, each failure is only temporary, and leads to an even greater success. E.g. after failing to secure a loan, one obtains an even larger one from another source. Or one who longs to be a distributor of a product fails to do so, but becomes an executive for the manufacturer. Consecrating or otherwise bringing the spirit to bear has this exceptional life response power.

Functioning from Spirit

Every human being has spirit inside but not fully aware of it. Spirit comes into our life as truth. When spirit surfaces in us, life will change its attitude to us. One can feel great enthusiasm and energy when the mind turns to spirit. Our own inner spirit can accomplish much more than our mind. Spirit is beyond body, mind, heart. We can make Time, Luck, Prosperity come into our life by functioning from spirit. Where man ends, the spirit begins.

Man energises his suffering by dwelling on it. Refusing to think of the problem will take us from mind to spirit. Spirit comes to the surface when the mind falls silent.

Commissioning spirit in life and functioning in Spirit brings infinite life response.

Mind works through trial and error. Spirit avoids labour and error. Spirit rushes into field WHEN

1. We take other person's point of view.
2. We don't react when offended.
3. We consider a wider ideal than our own selfish advantage.
4. Go to the inner silence.
5. We sympathise with the folly of the offender.

For Yoga, the spirit needs to remain on the surface forever.

Line of Evolution: Physical man, Mental man, Spiritual man

By using country plough one can't plough deeper than a few inches but a powerful tractor can plough many feet. Change of instrument changes the result.

What the physical man accomplished through use of hands and legs is exceeded by educated mental man through use of a tractor. Mind is a superior instrument which makes possible for an educated mental man what is impossible for an uneducated physical man. Spirit is a far superior instrument which makes possible what is impossible to mental man.

When spirit acts, we feel calm, joy, cheerfulness. Life will change its attitude to us. When we examine our life we can recollect some fortunate events which would have happened by themselves. We relate to our life by result, not the process by which result is arrived at. We miss such spirit- driven events. We hear in conversation, people exclaim, "Somehow, something happened and I got into IAS, otherwise I would have ended up as nobody somewhere."

Misfortune missed, luck seeking one are landmark events in anyone's life. Examining them will reveal the spirit in action, in our life events.

Spiritually conscious man-Shocks come to steel us in the right direction. Sometimes the Divine sanctions negative circumstances so that we can learn from that experience and grow as a person.

Growth is evolution from unconsciousness to consciousness.

- An infant is physically unconscious.
- Man is socially conscious.
- Thinker is mentally conscious.
- **Humanity** is **spiritually unconscious.**
- Emergence of psychic (**evolutionary soul**) makes man **spiritually conscious.**

Drishti to Drishta

Consciousness is in the attempt to make this world as Brahman (Supreme Absolute). When this CREATION becomes CONSCIOUS BRAHMAN, the aim of evolution to experience the DELIGHT (what Brahman experienced as BLISS in its Aloneness) will be fulfilled. Universe is supporting this evolution. Universe awakens itself through the individual centres. Man is the centre through which the Universe is trying to evolve and fulfill the evolutionary aim of Brahman.

Being (Brahman) has become the Creation. It is the Becoming. Realisation of Brahman in this Creation is realisation of the Being in the Becoming. It is the Being of the Becoming, which is none other than a psychic soul. Rather than Being, Becoming, Being of the Becoming is more powerful as it contains both Being and Becoming. But the first step towards it is to turn our gaze inward and become Drishta, the Witnessing Consciousness. We have to attain our Being.

As long as we remain as players in our life and spectators of others' lives, progress is limited. But the moment we turn our vision inside and look at our life as a spectator instead of a player, enormous progress in consciousness we can witness coupled with outer growth of our life. Unlimited TRANSFORMATION sets in when we turn ourselves from the act of SEEING, that is from the position of DRISHTI to WITNESSING consciousness, DRISHTA.

Like the sky behind the moving clouds, our consciousness is behind our moving thoughts. Even if clouds move away, the sky remains. Behind our clouds of moving thoughts, there is the sky of our consciousness. Consciousness is behind our thoughts. Gradually we have to shift from our temporary thoughts to permanent consciousness. Our attachment has to shift from temporary to permanent. We have to detach from temporary and attach to permanence. Our detachment to the lower is attachment to the higher. Our attachment has to be with the eternal and the eternal substance as Man is an eternal spiritual being. Shifting from Drishti to Drishta, we shift to Spirit.

Karma Vs. Spirit

Man can function from the Spiritual centre more effectively than his vital or mental centre. Our inner spirit emerges and dissolves our Karma. Karma is avoidable entirely if one lives in the Spirit. A life uninhibited by karma must be able to expand endlessly. By shifting to spirit we can shine our light.

By shifting to Spirit, trapped Energies, trapped Thoughts, trapped Financial life, etc turnaround to attract abundance and prosperity. Transformation, miracles happen upon removing the karmic imprint and we can access our natural gifts.

One is initiated to higher timeline and higher consciousness. We incorporate powerful creative routines in our life being in a Soul-flow state, create better inner space for ourselves, feeling spiritual, energetic, letting go of compulsive behaviours and thought patterns. We energetically align with our higher self.

The Secret is "Surrender, Allow, Flow"

The entire Universe and all our life movements and moments act as a GREAT AWAKENER in our EVOLUTION. A lifetime of thoughtful reading awaits us. This one birth lifetime is very brief when compared to the evolution we can make. Ego is the bar. Ego conceals our dependence on the Supreme Power of Existence, Consciousness, Delight. Dissolving ego paves way for dissolving the karma and to shift to spirit. When we shift to spirit, the evolution which we can make in several births can be attained in this one birth. Spirit makes it possible. Spirit abridges the time of our evolution and progress.

Expressions of Spirit

A sales manager tried to invoke the Spirit in his profession of sales and his performance skyrocketed. For another individual the invocation gave a great inner calm that was pleasant. These are the material and spiritual expressions of successful invocation.

Shifting to Spirit raises the Atmosphere

One's house may be disorderly or may even be dirty with cobwebs all over. Disorder and dirt will defy the Spirit. Such disorder and dirt absorbs the light of the spirit and stops prosperity moving towards us. Hence the importance of orderliness and cleanliness to raise the atmosphere of the place for full action of the Spirit. The house needs to be clean, clean by the highest possible standards. Orderliness is paramount. No shouting or loud voice is permissible. One must talk softly. The same principles apply to any place whether home or work place.

Levels of shifting to Spirit

Once we have decided to shift to Spirit and function from Spirit, the decision and our firm belief has to be endorsed by our emotions. We have to believe in our emotions that spirit is more powerful than mind. Right comprehension will strengthen the belief and calmness will begin to collect inside. Then gradually we can try to shift from thought to silence at each moment of acting. Life will pleasantly bend itself to your will. Then we can try to shift each thought into its higher counterpart of inner silence. It is a single minded inner work. We can try to stay in the new level of consciousness to gain firm footing in our inner being and to act from the inner centre by invoking the Spirit. A pool of silence collects inside which is an indication of the surfacing of Spirit. Silence is the atmosphere of inner spirit.

Ways for Shifting to Spirit

- Ceasing to reason
- To avoid all quarrels at home and office
- To write precise accounts
- Consecration
- Prayer
- Taking interest in daily work to organise an unorganised work
- To give thought to work which we are doing unthinkingly
- Take other man's point of view
- Cultivate patience and self giving
- Knowing past errors and avoid them in future

In life, the effects of our foolish acts are irreversible. In Spirit the effect of our past foolish acts can now be reversed if we reverse our attitude now in understanding and in our emotions deeply felt. Such reversal will fully dissolve the consequences and liberate us forever. Spirit corrects physical facts by reversal of true feelings deeply realised. A mountain of debts can dissolve into thin air if there is a mountain of felt emotions regretting it.

Once you see spirit responding to your call one must cultivate to build up your life, organise it so that it progresses.

Spirit's Power to untie the Guardian Knot in our being

Guardian Knot- We know the story. When Alexander visited the city of Gordium, he encountered an ancient wagon tied with an incredibly intricate knot. An oracle had proclaimed that whoever could unravel the knot would become the ruler of all Asia.

Instead of trying to untie the knot, Alexander boldly sliced through it with his sword, fulfilling a prophecy that he would become the ruler of all Asia.

Invoking the Spirit is like invoking the power to untie the Guardian knot of our swabhava and to raise the consciousness. Having faith in our knowledge and capacities we try to solve our problems one by one like untying a complicated knot. Shifting the faith in our capacities to faith in Spirit's capacities makes the Spirit to surface and untangle many knots of the problems at once and bring many opportunities which are at present unimaginable by us at one stroke. Our spirit has power to untie the Guardian Knot in our being and usher us to prosperity. Emerging SPIRIT gives us the strength to drop all the imaginary scaffoldings which we are unconsciously holding on to.

Spirit-oriented Expression, Spiritual Habits

Qualities of the Spiritual-Oriented Individual and Spirit-oriented Expression

The person who invokes constantly the Inner Spirit and functions from Spirit 's life is entirely different. It is a New way of Living. Such a person is no longer a child soul but a ripe soul in the process of becoming an evolutionary adult, on the sunlit path of evolution in Light and Delight and quickly climbs the evolutionary ladder. No more is progress tainted with suffering in ignorance but the progress is filled with joy in knowledge.

What will be the orientations and expressions of such an individual who lives by Spirit?

Here are some of the qualities and expressions of such Spiritual Individual.

1. Not resorts to physical punishment (e.g. against children by parents).
2. Not forces children to be like themselves.
3. Not preoccupied with the acquisition of private property.
4. Avoids rituals, focuses instead on self-giving, harmony, and love.
5. Does not idolise others based on their power and influence.
6. Seeks truth and new understanding instead of fame and personal recognition.
7. Feels no compulsion to broadcast themselves to others.
8. Not pushes and forces life, instead waits for life to come to him.

9. Relies on Life-initiatives instead of Self-initiatives on the understanding that Life's initiatives are wise and sustain than Self initiatives. Whatever comes on its own, sustains and benefits us.

10. Not asserts his position, but constantly learns from others.

11. Is not selfish, but consistently self-giving.

12. Avoids herd mentality and thinks independently.

13. Is not satisfied with a single truth, seeking to know the many sided truth of things.

14. Does not seek answers through cerebral labour or hard churning of thought, but through intuition.

15. Does not confine himself to ordinary views of time and space.

16. Is not satisfied with mechanistic view how life works and unfolds but looks beyond it.

17. Is not troubled by negativity, seeing the utility in negativity.

18. Is not constrained by limits of the society, as the individual sees beyond them from universal dimension.

19. Adheres to his own higher values than of the society.

20. Is not swayed or satisfied with others' opinions, but seeks the true Truth.

21. Is not satisfied with the visible alone, but values the subtle and invisible.

22. Sees the infinite in the finite.

23. Sees the logic of the infinite in the magic of the finite.

24. Avoids gossip, understanding its destructive potential.

25. Is not influenced by current outlooks, but takes a longer view.

26. Does not get swept away by the tide of emotions in events, seeks balance and truth instead.

27. Does not seek numerous friendships for their own sake.

28. Is oriented inwardly rather than outwardly.

29. Does not seek to be entertained, but to understand.

30. Does not seek superficial interactions, but deep connections through heart, higher mind, and spirit.

31. Seeks beauty and knowledge, not power.

32. Is not overly influenced by another's age, whether young or old.

33. Does not rebel for its own sake.

34. Does not obsess over sickness and illness, remaining calm, steady, and positive.

35. Is not agitated by broadcast opinions. Example -the media, as he avoids them.

36. Not reacts impulsively on urge to any person or situation but remains still, observant, and understanding.

37. Not seeks to perfect others, but to perfect himself.

38. Not offers unsolicited opinions, preferring to be still, wait, and learn.

39. Not attempt to advise others. Resorts to advise only when someone asks for the advice. Has the understanding that anyone hates unsought advice and such advice is not helpful and goes waste .

40. Does not seek short-term happiness, but long-term joy.

41. Is not prejudiced towards another in terms of their station and position.

42. Never feels condescending or superior, accepting all as equals.

43. Does not complain about others or life, choosing acceptance instead.

44. Does not blame others, but takes responsibility.

45. Accepts the present circumstances life has given him.

46. Avoids the surface and seeks the depths.

47. Strives for all qualities of spirit like harmony, oneness, truth, knowledge, goodness, creativity, love, beauty, and the delight of being.

48. Lives by consecration. Has the wisdom there is no joy than that of consecrated living.

49. Feels always energetic and cheerful due to ever living connection with the Spirit.

50. Heart filled with heavenly strengths and mass of courage, lives thrilled by Spirit's Light and Wisdom seeing the Spirit in Action .

Spiritual Habits

Here is list of spiritual habits one can practice to carry out the Inner work to grow within, increase the wisdom and consciousness, to acquire the power to move the Life from within.

1. Values and Practices

*Spirit-Oriented Works: Do work for the highest values imaginable, including service to the Divine.

*Goodness: Do good and act rightly in every situation.

*Self-Givingness: Move from selfishness to self-givingness, taking pleasure in the needs, interests, and successes of others, and showing genuine affection.

2. Attitudes and Interactions

*Generosity: Give fully and generously in terms of resources (time, effort, knowledge) whenever possible and appropriate.

*Goodwill: Extend goodwill to everyone you meet and come in contact with. Send goodwill to others through the atmosphere. Avoid goodwill to those who mean harm. Be neutral there.

*Humility: Avoid ego-related matters and self-aggrandisement.

*Gratitude: Feel deep appreciation for all or particular things that have come your way.

*Soft/Reduced Speech: Speak in a low, soft voice; use fewer words; Not interrupt others while speaking. Remain curious. Remain silent whenever possible. Listen with your Beingness and Presence.

*Silent Will: Hold back expression of one's thoughts and wishes, which will compel others to speak it out.

***Taking Another's Point of View:**   See the truth in others' words, regardless of differing perspectives.

***Patience:**   Resist the urge to hasten desired outcomes; Impatience should not touch the nerves.

3. *Inner Qualities*

***Equality of Being:**   Maintain calmness in the face of difficulties or when an intense positive arises in your life. Not to get excited and remain neutral.

***Inner Detachment (Non-reaction):**   Remain poised and non-reactive to others' actions or words, embracing non-reaction. Non-reaction is the first step for taking to Spirit. Not only outward, gradually the reaction to be stopped in one's inner too.

***Non-Initiating:**   Refrain from taking action unnecessarily, allowing powerful positive conditions to be attracted to you.

***Peace (Inner Spiritual):**   Move from outer disturbance to inner calm by consciously cultivating it and make peace your natural state.

***Opening to the Spiritual Force (Consecration):**   Seek the Divine's and Spirit's guidance before starting any activity or addressing problems or reversal of negative attitudes, to quickly gain life's cooperation.

***Moving to the Depths Within (Concentration):**   Centre yourself in the inner being and not on the outer surface. Peace, richness, right understanding, and positive life movements will become the norm rather than an exception.

***Living in the Now/The Ever-Present:**   Don't think about the past unless it is useful to the present. The same with the future. Unite past, present, and future through the right consciousness in the Eternal Now.

***Seeing Beyond the Positive & Negative:**   Recognise the utility of both good and bad, positive and negative, for life's and your progress.

***Seeing the Outer as a Reflection of the Inner:**   Understand that Life and Life's situations mirror your inner atmosphere. External circumstances reflect your inner consciousness. Improve the positive aspects in your inner and eliminate the negative to see favourable changes externally.

*****Inner Awareness of Subtle Forces:*** Develop awareness of the subtle forces of life unfolding around you, enhancing understanding, decision-making, and actions that enable favourable responses from life.

4. *Spiritual Aspirations*

*****Spiritual Sincerity:*** Aspire constantly for the Divine and Spirit to enter your life.

*****Surrender:*** Offer every act and your existence to fulfill the Divine's Intent and Will.

*****Mind's Movement Out of Ignorance:*** Acknowledge that the mind knows only a part, not the whole and seek the many sided truth for integral knowledge and accomplishment in life.

*****Power of Mind and Spiritual Mind:*** Mind depieces everything. For Integral knowledge you have to transcend the mind. Overcome the hard churning of thought to experience knowledge through silence, intuition, illumination, revelation, and integral perception. Achieve this through constant consecration and calling on the Divine and Spirit.

*****Faith (Spiritual):*** Shift your trust to the Divine and Spirit.

*Calling the Spirit: Try calling the Spirit into your life whenever possible, evoking its power for general or specific matters.

*****Seeing the Marvel:*** Perceive every event, positive or negative, as it arises, contributing to life's unfolding and progress. See the Divine's intention behind each of your life movements and moments.

*****Seeing the Infinite in the Finite:*** Realise that in the smallest things and finite, infinite can break out with infinite possibilities when you see everything in the right consciousness.

*****Break the Habit:*** Perform an act one or several levels higher. E.g. a physical act with emotion (vital); physical or vital act with thought (mentality); mental act with spiritual perception.

5. *Truth and Integrity*

***Truth:** Know the full truth of a thing, and act from the full truth of any matter. BE truthful and honest to gain life's cooperation.

***Values:** Apply your deepest values, such as tolerance, respect, and harmony, and adopt new values. Values are spiritual skills.

***Spiritual Values:** Embrace any of these universal spiritual expressions—Truth, Silence, Wisdom, Knowledge, Harmony, Oneness, Peace, Love, Beauty, Delight, Infinity, Timelessness—in increasing measure.

6. *Soul and Consciousness*

***Evolving Soul:** Seek the inner being, including the evolving soul within (psychic being) which will put you in touch with your highest nature and help you to live your soul's purpose in evolutionary growth.

***Resolve Contradictions into Harmony:** Resolve conflicts with another or other things or matters by discovering the higher harmony.

***Contradictions as Complements:** See the things you are in conflict with and divided from as actually true complements; that serves the purpose of your growth.

***Soul to Soul Connection:** By connecting to your soul, you connect with the soul of others, experiencing Inner Oneness and mutually helping each other in evolution consciously.

***Raise the Attitudes:** Constantly raise your level of attitudes, overcoming all wanting ones while maintaining a positive outlook.

***See Divine in Others:** Each time you meet with another, try to see them as the Divine. Respect them to that degree. In reality, it is the Truth of things.

82

Surrender

Without a transformation of mind and heart, realisation is unattainable. For Unity with the Divine, three things are required understanding of the mind, heart's surrender, life's obedience. Our ego perceives problems, whereas our psychic soul sees joy.

Surrender is giving up the drop of our egoistic existence in exchange for an ocean of infinite being and existence. Surrender is the conscious act of letting go and a deliberate attempt to surrender one's capacities and invoking the capacities of Spirit. It is to shift the faith in one's own capacities to the capacities of the Spirit. Surrender is conscious unconsciousness. Aspiration and Surrender both are required. To tune our will to Divine Will brings everything harmoniously in our life for evolution. Surrender is to be one with the flow of the Universe.

Outside it is labour; inside it is joy. Surrender is the link. Labour of the outside becomes the joy of the inside by surrender. We live in the past, enjoy it, call it nostalgia. To surrender the past is to conquer the future, to enrich the present into eternity. Surrender conquers Time.

Prayer-Gratitude-Surrender

Surrender is ultimate which encompasses prayer, gratitude and expands beyond. In short, surrender is submitting oneself to the Divine's WILL. In Prayer, there is expression of one's Will. Prayer is seeking the Divine for manifestation of something which may range from material to spiritual.

51

Prayer is the practical action for invoking the Divine and Spirit in the act. Gratitude is primarily the inward recognition, acknowledgement of the manifestation.

In Gratitude, as there is acknowledgement, it too carries subtle expressions of one's Will. Whereas in Surrender, the Highest form, there is no Individual's Will. Only the Divine 's Will.

Personality and Surrender

The centre of personality decides the scope of surrender. Surrender is limited by our centre. Surrender converts the greatest tragedy in the gross plane through subtle and causal planes into the greatest opportunity. Surrender walks through the subtle into the causal. Surrender makes the idiot realise that he is a genius. As we can board a plane without knowing anything as a user, we can enter into Spiritual consciousness as a process of surrender.

Surrender is Spirit

Surrender is the soul's awakening to its origin. Surrender is to give up the energies and give up the capacities to discipline the impulses. The most certain and direct way to understand something is through identification with it. It is a direct knowledge which comes through the power of identification. This identification is attained by surrender to the thing. Surrender gives direct knowledge. One can learn from genius. It is limited. But by identification with the genius, we get all faculties of the genius. By identification with our Inner Spirit through surrender, we get all wisdom and powers of the Spirit. It is the most effective way for evolution but most difficult too because surrender calls for gathering all our constantly outbound energies inside and using it to transform our lower nature and offer to our inner flame of aspiration to consecrate and surrender to the Spirit. Aspiration is followed by Concentration, Consecration, Surrender. Surrender is graded. Much inner work must be done to attain the state of Surrender.

There is a saying that "Only the like can surrender to the like." To surrender to the Spirit, one has to become the All-flaming Spirit itself in one's inner.

Surrender is the soul's awakening to its origin. It involves relinquishing energies and capacities to discipline impulses. The most certain and direct way to understand something is through identification with it, bypassing the need for complex science. This direct knowledge arises from the power of identification, which is achieved through surrender to the object of understanding.

Surrender is the expression of the soul. What we cannot do on our own, life brings pressure for us to do for our growth. What life forcefully sends to us for our growth, if we choose to voluntarily self-will and aspire to put efforts for our growth, the struggle will be very much lesser.

Our surface mind thinks what we are doing is right and others are wrong whereas our subliminal mind knows it to be wrong. When surface mind turns to the subliminal mind and the realisation comes on the surface mind the thing what we are doing is wrong, opening arises and realisation, transformation comes on us.

Ultimate Evolutionary Aim of Surrender-To serve as Divine Instrument in experiencing Enriched Delight of Existence

Consecration involves opening ourselves to the Higher Power to bring its Force into the details of our lives. Surrender is the highest form of consecration which requires us to offer our entire being and existence as instruments of the Divine.

Why should we surrender our very existence to the Higher Power, fully follow Its Will, and be receptacles for Its Intent? Understanding our role within the larger context of Reality might compel us to surrender with greater intensity and frequency.

In "The Life Divine," Sri Aurobindo discusses a Transcendent Will that created the universe to manifest Its Real Ideas in endless multiplicity and to experience the Delight in Existence what the Transcendent experiences as Bliss in its solitude. As conscious individuals, we serve as instruments of this Divine Will, enabling the universe to fulfill its destiny by actualising the Intent of the Transcendent.

Surrender, in this context, has profound significance. By fully opening to our psychic being and the spiritual Force, we become "Informed" of our spiritual duty and role. Through personal growth and accomplishments aligned with this duty, we serve a broader cosmic purpose, fulfilling the Transcendent's Intent and realising It's Real Ideas.

By surrendering to the Divine Force, we discover our Highest Purpose and are increasingly inclined to act accordingly. Life responds overwhelmingly to such alignment. Even without fully understanding our purpose, surrendering in pure faith can have a profound effect.

Reflecting on these issues and considering our current and potential roles in the world, we find that through surrender, our highest Role becomes clearer. The strategies and specifics reveal themselves, guiding us on how to be and act.

The intensity of our surrender and our receptivity will determine our ability to fully align with the Cosmic Intent of the Transcendent Divine. If we succeed, we will serve well as collaborators of the Infinite, increasingly realising and fulfilling our individual Destiny in the world.

Power of Surrender to reverse the outer situation instantaneously-Ray's Surrender in Classroom

One day several years ago, Ray was conducting a training class. However, unlike his other courses, the morning session of this class had gone horribly. Every imaginable problem showed up: Students came late; Ray consistently stumbled in his presentation; the students argued a lot; he became defensive; and so forth. It was the worst possible scenario faced by Ray.

Because the class had gone so horribly that morning, Ray was not eager for the afternoon session. However, luckily, Ray was able to observe himself and control his anxiety. He then made the inner, psychological effort to reverse the situation. Ray relaxed, turned his focus inward, and then surrender the situation -the remainder of the class to the spiritual Force. He said something like, "I don't know what to do now, but I know that if I leave the situation in your hands, everything will be fine. It has to!" Then he returned to class for the afternoon and taught as usual.

Within a half hour or so, Ray noticed a considerable change in the tone and atmosphere of the class. One thing he noticed was that all of the students arrived on time after lunch break which was unusual based on previous experiences. Second, he noticed how smoothly and effortlessly each lesson progressed, with each part of his performance fitting perfectly into the next, creating a beautiful harmonious rhythm. Thirdly, he noticed that the students were now not only calm and composed, but completely focused on their studies - a complete turnaround from the morning session. In fact, when Ray attempted to engage them in conversation, they were not only responsive but warm and friendly. This in turn forced him to express his own appreciation for their participation and contribution. Finally, he noticed how free the session was from outside distractions, allowing the class to flow smoothly and without interruption.

In all his years of instruction, Ray had never seen such a turnaround. It was almost as if he had stepped out of training torture and entered instructional heaven. And he was able to make this amazing transition by surrender himself and the situation up to the spiritual power. Through an act of intense consecration and surrender, he transformed an extremely disturbed and turbulent situation into one of calm, harmony and focused energy. By opening to the Higher Power, Ray was able to bring life completely under control. In this case, he opened to the spiritual Force—

i.e., consecrated in a difficult situation— and miraculously it got turned around.

Benefits of Surrender

When we engage in the act of surrender, any of an array of startling conditions can present themselves. Among them:

- Positive circumstances appear out of nowhere
- Solutions to Problems Are Suddenly Revealed
- Negative Situations Quickly Vanish
- Feelings of Richness and Joy Are Experienced
- The Unexpected and Creative Become the Norm
- A Deep Knowledge and Truth of Things Dawns in Our Inner
- Increase in Understanding of Spirit's Force and Action
- In Essence, Life Comes Under Our Control.

Part VI

LIFE, LIFE RESPONSE, LIFE CHARACTER

— from 'Savitri' by Sri Aurobindo

LIFE

Life is Force. Force is Power. Power is Will. Will is the working of the Master Consciousness.

Life is an AWAKENER for us. The key purpose of life is to increase our awareness, to make us evolve and manifest the hidden Spirit. Life brings to us the progress we need to make.

The whole universe is trying to move towards higher consciousness. Without the impact of Life we'll be left in inertia and will remain unchanged like the animal kingdom. Whether it brings us a positive or a negative depends on the level of our development and our response to life.

Life is a play of subtle universal forces which is in equilibrium. Behind the Life energy, there is a WILL. The energy of Life is an expression of WILL. Life acts at every moment to preserve and restore equilibrium.

Where the force for evolutionary change or aspiration is weak, life overcomes it and restores the equilibrium at the present level. If the force for change is strong, it disrupts the equilibrium at the present level. Hence life rises to restore the equilibrium at a higher level.

Herein lies the significance of our aspiration for growth.

Life-Reaction Vs. Life-Response

If our consciousness becomes low, life provokes us by outer circumstances to go back to our earlier state and thereby restores the equilibrium. If our consciousness is aspiring to climb higher, life responds to us by bringing positive life situations and collaborating in our growth for us to climb in our consciousness. In the first case, it is Life-Reaction which is NEGATIVE. In the second case, it is Life-Response which is POSITIVE.

In other words, we can say that Life always acts to restore equilibrium. Normally it reacts to restore the status quo at the present level of our existence. But when we elevate our consciousness to a higher level, it responds to elevate the life around us to that same level, thereby restoring the balance at a higher level. _Routine actions generate reactions from life and progressive actions evoke responses._

FORCE-CONSCIOUSNESS-ORGANISATION

Our capacity to accomplish is infinitely multiplied by shifting from the outer to the inner.

Life evolves by consciousness. Consciousness evolves by organisation.

Contact of form with form releases force. Contact of force with force releases consciousness.

Science regards life as inanimate force, energy in motion, which lacks consciousness or intention. But the force of life is conscious. Consciousness is inherent in the force. Consciousness is involved in the force and seeks to emerge. The contact and conflict of force with force in life releases the hidden consciousness within it, enabling life to evolve to a higher level.

Character of Life

As long as we understand life events as reflections of what we are, we will have the power to accomplish anything and overcome any difficulty.

The events of our lives appear to lack coherence due to a limitation in our understanding. Those who perceive the true character of life realise that it has a complete connected significance.

Life has a character. Everything has a character—objects, plants, animals, people, countries, languages. Life is the one thing that appears to have no clear and consistent pattern. We often hear the phrase life is like that, which means that life is unpredictable and inexplicable. The word CHARACTER implies structure and pattern. A person with character is one who acts in predictable ways, regardless of the situation.

However, this is exactly the opposite of how life events seem to behave. They are unpredictable. No matter what we do, no matter how hard we try, we can never foresee or explain the intervention of chance, whether in the form of luck or misfortune.

In fact, behind the apparently fickle behaviour of life there is a concealed structure, pattern, a formula, a law. There are no chance occurrences. Everything happens according to the laws of life.

There is a mechanism connecting events and the correspondence. The correspondence is Inner-Outer correspondence governed by the Life mechanism. Hence, Life is a dynamic play of a universal Energy, a Conscious Force, that builds and maintains the world.

Life Response

Life Response is a phenomenon where individuals experience sudden positive changes after altering their consciousness. It often goes unnoticed but can be **consciously invoked** by understanding the life mechanism and applying the right inner and outer behaviours that attract miraculous-like results. For instance, overcoming a negative attitude might lead to the sudden disappearance of an ongoing problem.

Life response is based on life's realities. One grows wiser by learning of these realities. We can train ourselves to see Life-truths in daily activities.

Example

Once a person felt a strong urge to visit his long-lost friend. Just as he was about to leave, he was told that someone, a stranger, had come looking for him. He went out to see who it was. To his surprise it was the friend whose house he was preparing to go to. The friend's arrival was in response to his longing. This is not chance or coincidence, but a rule of life, it is a Life Response.

Life Response represents that idea about the movements of life.

Life Responds not only to real thoughts, but also to imaginary, illusory thoughts. A man was **complaining** scores of times a day that he was **exploited by everyone** while there was nothing to exploit. This created an inner pressure in him that he compelled a few to exploit him. Everyone can recollect many such incidents in life.

Life has its rules. It holds itself in equilibrium. Life is a field of energy organised according to a system. It is life energy, not physical energy or mental energy. Life energy holds itself in an equilibrium. When the equilibrium is changed or disturbed, as in a fully automated factory, it restores itself. The restoration of the equilibrium necessitates a fresh act. The fresh act is the response of Life - a Life Response.

Life Responses are positive, negative or neutral. Life has a character. Life Response has its own special characteristics. A positive move gives rise to a positive Life Response. A negative move gives place to a negative Life Response. Our epics, history, fiction, and world literature are full of life responses. Even fables, parables, and simple stories too honour the rules of Life Response. We can make Life Respond. ***Life acts as if it is a person and it has a personality.*** The truth is life does have a personality and we are one life point of the fabric of life. Life responds by a beneficial, miraculous act when the equilibrium of emotions is restored.

There is no need to feel sorrow - for something done or left undone, an opportunity seemingly lost - *__all happens for the soul's swiftest evolution.__*

Life is one of expansive JOY, not a punishment of karma. Karma is avoidable entirely if one lives in the Spirit. Karma can be overcome by mental illumination. Life is not final. Mind is greater than life. Spirit is greater than mind. Life exists in spirit. Spirit is the centre of life. As Spirit is enthroned in life, invoking spirit brings greatest life response. Experiencing Spirit in life is the descent of the divine and it is the divine life. A life uninhibited by karma must be able to expand endlessly.

To us life is an evil whereas it is a plane of existence. Life is in pursuit of delight.

Sat-Chit-Ananda is Existence-Consciousness-Delight.

Sat-Chit-Ananda created the world for Delight.

Existent (Being) puts forth the Existence (Becoming) through Conscious-Force for experiencing Delight. Everything in the universe seeks self-delight. Delight comes by self- expression. When this self- expression is restricted or hurt, one feels the pain.

Pain is a restricted delight. When pain is intense, one calls it evil.

Each pain has secret widening power. There is deep Delight hidden behind each pain.

Pain makes for fuller enjoyment of Delight.

Problems have their solutions in-built into them. The outer is a reflection of the inner. The consequences of how we think are faithfully mirrored back by the outside world. The universe is a perfect feedback device. What we think is what we get. If we want to change the world, we must first change ourselves. We must explore and change our internal experience if we are to influence and shape the external world with wisdom.

Life, business, work, family, fortune can expand infinitely. Life is full of opportunities.

We are unconscious. We have to move from unconsciousness to consciousness. Life is not limited by death. We grow by giving. Self-giving is the basis of this life, not selfishness.

Experience is **not what happens** to us. It is **what we do with what happens** to us. The results of our actions come back to us in a loop.

Law is a relationship between events. The laws have behind them principles or Truths.

One should learn, observe, organise the thoughts, see the results, emphasise learning, NOT the results and WAIT for results to sail towards him. **One who honours this rule, will meet with unending progress.**

A man follows his inclinations, impulses, urges and exhausts them in the course of which he enjoys. For him, life reacts with low income, tension, violent enjoyment and their direct consequences. One cannot be moral here but must study the play of laws exactly. In case he wishes to attain high income, peace of mind, quiet, rich smooth enjoyment, the very same laws will instruct him accordingly.

The Determinant and Endless Expansion

To the Man who is unawakened, life is the determinant. Life determines him.

To the Man who is awakened, life lends its power for use. Man determines his life.

- Man can function from the Spiritual centre more effectively than his vital or mental centre.
- One has to outgrow social, moral limitations.
- Harmony is the secret of accomplishment.

- A business can endlessly expand if it is willing to constantly upgrade its organisation.

- Life at home can be full of joy and cheerfulness, completely without problems.

- We can attain any level of wealth we choose.

- Body can cure itself.

- Natural forces and the social environment are under man's control.

- There is no evil, falsehood, or sin in life for those who have come out of the ego.

- For egoless people, difficulties are opportunities and contradictions are complements.

If all of the above are true, what does it mean for one in domestic life or business life? It means, in the measure one emerges out of ego, one can have a life of joy and abundance at home. A business can survive and grow without the interference of the government, strikes and market conditions.

Challenges met in the right spirit must lead to an expansion. One can succumb to it or face the challenge with cheerfulness. We can choose to embrace a higher life, a life of Truth, a life of prosperity, a life free from pain and suffering.

An intelligent man learns from his own experience; wise man from the experiences of others.

There is always corresponding inner development to the outer new events in our life.

Great moment for our inner transformation is the moment when our temperament is on the edge. Life touches us at the tether end of our personality. When we feel hurt it is wise to observe the life response which is trying to teach us something. Our surface life is a diminished representation of our greater existence. When one has great inner potential, life refuses to fulfill one's desires. It is the life's way of applying pressure to exert and manifest the potentials of that person. FAILURE can be a great avenue for progress.

"Character of Life" explains the subtle reasons beyond the surface happenings.

When we are ready inside, life brings us the connections we need that will take us to the next level. At every moment life is bringing us what we need for our progress.

Every problem that comes into your life secretly serves as a means for you to grow.

If we insist more on this absolute truth, our self-awareness and life-awareness increases.

Reality inherent in this Creation and Life are discoverable. Assuming it as undiscoverable, the world is termed as Maya and illusion. The **world and life need not be shunned** and renounced as an illusion. It is **our ignorance which is to be renounced** for discovery of Reality.

Our life experiences remain as experiences. Most of our past life experiences are remaining in our memory as events waiting for us to draw the lessons, the life wisdom, the essence behind the appearances, to convert into valuable pearls of wisdom and to bring about the change in our personality, values and consciousness. Till such experiences are assimilated, transformed for our further evolution and the inner work is done, life forces us to see and keeps on repeating the same experiences though in different forms at various intensities till we learn the lessons from our life experiences. This is the secret of the law of life and the life response.

How to make life respond positively to us?
What is the secret law?

Secret law behind the Life Response

When we respond positively to life, life responds positively to us.

The magnitude of our response determines the magnitude of life response. It is very important for shifting to our inner and examine our response to life in thoughts, emotions, acts. When motives, attitude, perceptions are uplifted higher and become more positive, one cannot stop growth in one's life.

If we understand the significance in insignificance, if our motives, attitude, perception towards others and life changes positively, if we take conscious responsibility and take charge of ourselves and our life without laying back as victim, then we start realising all our life movements and challenges are really opportunities for our growth. One has to feel in the heart centre the need for growth. Then the eyes of the heart open and we stop blaming and start responding positively to life and life in turn responds to us positively. This is the secret law behind the life response.

Life experiences and knowledge alone is not enough, it has to be received in our emotions and vital to become part of our personality. It has to be possessed by us.

When we understand the concept of life response and start seeing the life response in our life, that is the point where we start talking to the Universe and also that is the point where we become conscious of the Universe talking to us.

This is the major point of transition which makes our life lively each moment. One analogy will explain better.

The difference will be like the world seen by caterpillar and the world seen by butterfly. The crawling caterpillar which sees hardly a few inches of the space of its existence, upon metamorphosis when it becomes butterfly, the freedom it experiences and its vision which spans the extensive space by flying. This is the difference between life leading us and we leading life. Life will be filled with meaning each moment.

To be frank, when we become conscious of our inner being and life response, the difference will be as though the caterpillar is given the eyes of man.

Work is what one does inwardly on one's character and attitude. Working on oneself helps unlocking treasure of set of values, and discovery of values can lead to inner expansion, higher capacity, enhances vitality and helps one to be in the TRULY BEST STATE.

Man knows all problems are of disharmony and therefore he seeks the solutions in harmony, not in outer harmony that needs long periods of preparation but in inner harmony. All problems of man are created by his reactions, ignorance, unconsciousness, superstition, and lack of organisation. So he moves to inner equality, inner comprehension to master outer ignorance, inner awakening of consciousness, inner clarity of actual information instead of bogus impressions that foster fertile superstitions. Thus he moves to overcome situations created by the lack of organisation outside in life and he organises himself inside.

Life is Neutral

Life progresses through good as well as evil, says Sri Aurobindo. Justice lies at the end of a quarrel. Good is a shining part, but still a part. Life is bigger than good or evil.

Life is a whole. Life to become complete needs good as well as evil.

If water supply is essential, the sewage system is equally essential. One completes the other. We like the good part, dislike the bad one. Life will not be complete in the absence of falsehood or evil. This is the **character of human life.** When it is complete, it ceases to be human life. It becomes a higher life. The fine play that is performed on stages is made conceivable by the green room that is clumsy and scattered behind, which cannot be shown.

There are people who exclaim, "God is great. He always protects me. I cannot survive without such divine protection. At the time of inspection, 70% of my work was unfinished. I would have been undone if the inspecting officers had ever come my way. The point is none of them came to my section." These people go scot-free and they boast over it. There are others who leave 1% of their work half finished having different experience.

They say, "I don't know what it is. Any inspecting authority never fails to visit my section. He goes straight to the file left unfinished, and every time I am the inescapable victim. It is my fate."

The progress of an honest man is in his honest work being perfect. Hence life picks at his imperfections. Life responds based on one's inner being and level of evolution and not based on one's behaviour or outer act. Life responds as per the need of one's current state of evolution and the person's timeline in the evolutionary ladder.

Why Do I Suffer?

We admire goodness and frown upon bad people. Our mind expects that good people should flourish and bad people should suffer. Out of negligence, a person gets an electric shock. It is not a punishment for the person's sins but simply ignorance. It is punishment for one's ignorance.

One gives a big sum to a cheat and lost the money. It is due to ignorance. One earned far more than his relatives and foolishly disclosed all his assets, thinking he is being honest. His relatives joined together and compelled him to give the best part of his cash assets. He yielded. Later they suddenly turned around and declared that none of them is going to return it. Also, they humiliated him by saying what a simpleton he was.

Those who earn money must also know how to protect it; otherwise, they become vulnerable. Life teaches through experiences, punishing ignorance and incapacity. The simple truth of life is that the strength of a weak man attracts unusual suffering from other strong people. He who cannot swim enters the water and drowns. The water does not warn you. It is dumb. If one man dies, the other men learn. For life, all men are one. We certainly do not commit such simple follies. But life is in layers of increasing strength. For anyone there is the next higher level. There he is bound to err, or suffer serious consequences.

Every individual faces challenges, and invoking spirit prevents such losses. When invoked, Spirit acts through life and He is guided to a good lawyer, capable doctor; he is given an excellent wife, endearing children. They are the ways of Grace. The action of the Spirit is Grace. It is our choice to keep the contact constant.

SECRET: Going Beyond the book 'The Secret'

The core idea behind "The Secret" is that our intentions can attract what we desire, mainly through visualisation and positive emotions, not having any expectations of what form the result will take, and waiting for the universe to respond. The Secret concludes that if you take this approach, the "Law of Attraction" will take over and quickly evoke your object of desire. This is indeed a profound understanding of the subtle nature of life.

However, while "The Secret" presents a simple method for manifestation, it lacks detailed explanations of **how and why it works**. In contrast, Life Response not only outlines the process but also delves into the underlying principles behind it.

"The Secret" focuses primarily on a single approach, i.e. visualise what you hope to achieve; aspire deeply for it (with your emotions in full support), and the universe will do the rest. Life Response recognises that reality is more complex. It acknowledges the importance of understanding various factors such as individual psychology, social and environmental contexts, and subtle laws of life. Life Response fills in those missing pieces with a range of methods to attract desired outcomes in any circumstance.

Finally, and perhaps most importantly, life response is not only a means of attracting success, **but addresses our entire nature, showing the way for complete fulfillment in life.** Where The Secret seeks to accomplish an objective, Life Response **seeks realisation at all levels of our being – material, psychological, social, and spiritual.**

After all, life is so vast, with infinite possibility and potential. Not only can we attract a targeted goal, such as a better job, but we can also experience the wonders of existence. In essence, Life Response provides a comprehensive understanding that encompasses every aspect of human nature.

All problems of life are problems of Harmony

The Infinite Power of Harmony

Wherever harmony is created, great energy and power is released.

When we embrace another person's point of view, holding back our own viewpoint, it is actually a movement toward harmony with that other party. When we overcome our mental limitations, preferences, rigid low nature, and embrace another's position, we move towards harmony.

Spiritually speaking when we shift from a separative ego consciousness to our inner being, we establish a harmonic connection with others and the world. The journey from a separative ego consciousness to a state of harmony is indeed a central theme in many spiritual traditions. As we connect with our inner being, we begin to perceive the interconnectedness of all life. Living in harmony involves aligning our actions, thoughts, and intentions with the principles of unity, love, and compassion. It means prioritising cooperation over competition, service over self-interest, and understanding over judgment.

Harmony not only creates better relationships with others but also energises the atmosphere in such a way making it easier for us to align with positive circumstances. In other words, any movement away from our own egoistic separative selves to one of achieving harmony with others or with life tends to bring about sudden good fortune.

Harmony-Spirit's Power

There are a number of expressions of the Spirit in life like Silence, Beingness, Truth, Wisdom, Timelessness, Infinity, Goodness, Love, Beauty, and Delight. Perhaps the most fundamental and essential among these is Harmony, which, at its highest expression, manifests as Oneness and Unity of being.

In the Infinite consciousness, all things are interconnected in essential Harmony and Oneness. Yet, from this essential Unity, an infinitely diverse universe was created, including us humans. This principle of underlying Harmony applies not only to Universe but to our individual and collective lives as well. When we bring greater harmony to express through our relationship with others and the world, we generate a vast creative power for accomplishment for ourselves and others.

Harmony strengthens the positive bonds between people and things, focusing energy and releasing power for accomplishment. We can see this in large-scale events like the formation of nations, as well as in everyday situations such as our work experiences. For example, reflect on your experience of workplace meetings. The most successful meetings often result from a deeper connection and bond among the team members-through mutual respect, genuine appreciation of others' contributions, and collaborative decision-making for future actions. After such meetings, our energy skyrockets leading to remarkable work outcomes. Essentially, the harmonic movement has created a new burst of collective energy now shared by each participant, enabling individual and collective achievement. Interestingly that success often comes about through instances of sudden good fortune.

Similarly, any two individuals can create this kind of harmonic bond. For example, increased harmony in romantic relationships can lead to the deepest form of love between partners. When each lover is willing to forget themselves, adoring the other for its own sake can generate a tidal wave of romantic energy resulting in an intense bond and affection that can last a lifetime.

The opposite of harmony happens when each party moves in its own direction, prioritising and focusing on their own self-interests at the expense of the needs of the "Other." This self-centred approach attracts negative life conditions. Growing aware of the presence of conflict and contradictions in one's inner landscape and reversing it to create alignment with others-spouse, family members, colleagues at work place, friends, business partners, clients etc attracts prosperity, abundance, joy in one's life.

Evolutionary Journey-Inconscient Matter to Superconscient Spirit

The Supreme Reality has created this universe with a Self-Conscious Being (Sat-Chit-Ananda) at one end and the Inconscient at the other, providing Itself with a field of Play, Lila, which is intrinsically Himself. The Superconscient has **self-willingly** lost itself and became Inconscient. This is Involution. The Superconscient Spirit which is **All-Knowing, All-Consciousness, All-Bliss** through Involution **became its opposites** as Inconscient Matter - Negating its Knowledge, Consciousness, Bliss and plunging in **Darkness, Ignorance, Pain and Suffering.** Through evolution, the Inconscient Matter which is the starting point of evolution aiming to become the other end of existence, i.e. Superconscient Spirit. Thus **evolution** initially happens **through the mode of oppositions, contradictions, conflicts.** This is the principle of creation. The same principle which is applicable to Absolute Supreme and Eternal is equally applicable for the universe and individual as well. The universe and individuals too evolve by contradictions and opposites. Oppositions to be reconciled and through reconciliation, harmony to be established.

OPPOSITION-RECONCILIATION-HARMONY is the formula

Sri Aurobindo says 'Turn everything to Honey.' Matter and Spirit are two extreme ends of Existence. Matter is not a contradiction or opposite of Spirit. Matter is an inherent Spirit. The apparent contradictions are inherent complements. All of our life and life experiences are happening for our evolution, for our growth in consciousness. People whom we associate with are agents for our growth. Through life situations, though people seem to oppose and contradict us, from a higher perspective and evolutionary point, these people and the situations are the best complements for our inner growth and taking us to higher harmony and unity with our inner self and Creation. The proportion in which we can develop this subtle perception about life and life events, our suffering and struggle will diminish and we start collaborating with life by aligning with life-force and life- intention from greater inner harmony which in turns brings greater outer harmony in life as well. It is only man who can reconcile the Spirit and Life. The GREAT SECRET OF HARMONY LIES IN RECONCILIATION. The Eternal creates infinite vibrations in the Individual. Infinity and infinite harmony is created by the opposites being reconciled.

Contradiction to Harmony

Every act in life turns out to be a complement for one who does not act on the Spirit of Contradiction. A common aspect has the essential hint for discovering the unity of the parts. Understanding the common aspect between two or more parts and reconciliation gives us realisation. In the unity of the parts is where the power of the whole lies. If you want to fly higher, you have to drop the things that weigh you down.

The truth is we live in this world. But the greater truth is the world lives in us.

There is no illusion. There is only ignorance. The inner gap in comprehension is expressed as an outer disappointed romance or a disappointed life. Man acts within the radius of his perceptions.

He commits folly when he acts outside the radius. Man is infinite in his potentials but finite in his expressions, interests and experiences.

All problems of life are problems of harmony. Essentially, the disharmony is also within ourselves. What our inner being seeks, our outer being repels. There is disharmony between our depths and surface. What is seen by our mind as shock, struggle, suffering in life is seen by Supreme consciousness as harmonious emergence of inner possibilities. What is seen by the mind as contradictions are seen as complements in Supreme Consciousness.

Contradictions are complements. Negative is hidden positive. Shifting from human perception to divine perception we shift from outer to inner, negative to positive.

Making an inner shift, we progress and accomplish in inner and outer.

The opposition seeks more harmony. Problems arise as long as we are in the Force and not in the Being. The surface mind alternates between problems and solutions while it permanently resides in an atmosphere that generates problems. A problem arises when we do not have the required skill or capacity permanently.

Despite our efforts to solve it, the problem often resurfaces because we lose the skill over time. If we possess permanent skills or capacity related to a problem, it would never arise again. For instance, during World War II, the British succeeded in breaking a certain German code and were ready to attack successfully. The German attack stopped forever. The presence of adequate equipment can prevent emergencies. The reappearance of a problem indicates the transience of the equipment or skills in addressing it. Treating the cause of the diseases and not the symptoms will bring permanent cure. Understanding and addressing the root-cause is essential. Our level of personality and consciousness determines the way we perceive the situation and the pace we resolve the problems.

Raising the levels of consciousness

Consciousness is the key for everything. Human consciousness can be categorised into three primary levels: Physical, Vital, and Mental. Each of these levels can be further subdivided into three parts: physical, vital, and mental, resulting in a total of nine levels. We refer to these as Levels 1 to 9. We each exist and live on all nine levels, but some levels are more developed and prominent than others with one level typically being predominant.

The majority of individuals, even those who are very intelligent and well educated, tend to primarily live at the physical and vital levels of consciousness. Only a select few truly Centre their lives on the mental plane. Living in a higher plane than the mental is rare and reserved for exceptional individuals. Spiritual progress involves continuously trying to raise our consciousness from the physical level to the mental level and beyond.

Physical- At the physical level, we are identified with our bodies and perceive ourselves as physical beings. Our consciousness is physical. We know the world through the five senses. Our concerns revolve around meeting physical needs and seeking pleasures. However, this is just one aspect of our existence; it serves as the base and foundation for our life in the world.

Vital- Yet, we are not just material beings. We are also vital beings capable of interacting with other people and cultivating positive relationships. Transitioning from the physical centre to the vital Centre elevates our consciousness. We become more alive, energetic and dynamic. Our focus shifts from mere survival and comfort to expansion, achievement, and adventure. We become curious, brave, and generous.

Mental- The mental consciousness is rooted in our ability to know, think, understand, and perceive. It surpasses the levels of physical and vital consciousness. It seeks knowledge. It is capable of accepting ideals and striving for perfection. When we shift to the mental consciousness, we spend **less time and energy in doing things** and **more for understanding ourselves, our lives, and how we can accomplish more**. We become better organised and more efficient, more creative, imaginative, innovative, tolerant, and also exhibit greater individualism and idealism in our thoughts and actions.

Above the mind there is a plane of higher mental consciousness in which we receive knowledge in silence without any mental effort or activity. To move up the scale of human consciousness and to outgrow each lower level, here are some ways to do -

To outgrow physicality

- Avoid seeking more physical comfort and convenience.
- Seek to make progress at every moment.
- Whatever you do physically, do it carefully and perfectly.
- Try to increase one level higher the physical values such as cleanliness, orderliness, punctuality, regularity, accuracy and quality.

To outgrow vitality

- Not to insist on doing only the things you like or are interested in.
- Take interest in everything you do.
- Never gossip, blame, complain.
- Never lose your temper or self-control.
- Reducing the amount of talking you do and learning to speak softly.

To outgrow mentality and become spiritual

- To think before you speak and act.
- Not just repeat what you know or have heard.
- Be open to new ideas.
- Not to insist on your own ideas and beliefs.

- Learn to listen to others.
- Learn to take the viewpoint of other people.
- Learn to see the other side – there is always truth in the opposite viewpoint.
- Learn to quiet the mind and receive knowledge in silence.
- Learn to go within, to concentrate deep within and behind one's heart in the psychic Centre which is full of peace, love and joy.

Signs of spiritual progress

How do we know when we are growing spiritually? Here are some of the indications:

Patience: We are more patient and tolerant.

Peace: We feel more calm and peaceful, even in the midst of other people and intensity activity.

Silence: Our minds become settled. Thoughts are no longer insistent. We may even experience periods in which the mind is completely still.

Equality: We do not react to disturbing events. We are capable of greater equanimity. We have the capacity to remain undisturbed without being indifferent.

Knowledge: We understand the significance of all experiences that come to us and know how to grow or outgrow the need for them.

Goodwill: We feel joyful in the joy of others. We no longer feel jealousy, resentment, or competition at the success of others.

Self-giving: We identify with others and aspire for their fulfillment more than for our own.

Joy: We feel a quiet, causeless happiness, a sense of contentment, an inner rich fullness that remains with us at all times.

By raising our consciousness, we gain the capacity to create more harmony with our inner self, towards life, others. More consciousness brings more harmony.

Avoidance Harmony vs. True Harmony

Often we choose to avoid situations, such as in meeting others, when we expect disturbance of harmony or eruption of contradictions and conflicts. But this is not true harmony but avoidance harmony. It is easy to step back from disharmony and avoid it. However it is better to find the inner limitation in one's self and change it, or discover the related inner change necessary that matches another's' negativity, or understanding the necessary inner changes required to align with the perspectives of others. Either way, we develop the inner strength to move to the resolution of the contradiction. Additionally, life tends to respond positively to our proactive efforts.

Transitioning from avoidance-based harmony to genuine harmony attracts profound results, as it addresses the root causes of discord rather than merely sidestepping them.

When we seek harmony, mutually beneficial outcome in any life situation rather than the selfish outcome at the expense of others, life tends to cooperate.

Seeking Harmony Rather than Win-Attracts Startling Resolutions After Decades of Dragging Dispute

Seeking harmony rather than victory led to a surprising resolution after decades of legal battles. The 6 member family was embroiled in a 55-year litigation over a significant property dispute. Despite initial victories and setbacks in various courts, the case persisted. Although M who was the youngest member of the family was not directly involved in the conduct of cases, M was very much upset & concerned & got fed-up. M being the last son & brother, M knew nobody would listen to his views. M was leaving for Iran on a very short assignment in a paper mill as a specialist. M wanted to put a full stop to this long dragging case. Finally, M decided to consecrate the issue to the Spirit with a prayer for a favourable outcome that would not harm either party but would resolve the matter amicably.

M's prayer was - "The case should be to our favour, but at the same time no party to be affected & should be settled amicably & harmoniously. " M left for Iran. When on M's brother's birthday, M greeted him, to his surprise & his family, the Supreme Court had given the judgement in favour of them, awarding a meager grant to the opposite party & settled the matter once for all. This is the life response entire M's family received by M's sincere aspiration for harmony.

Higher harmony in company, business or any organisation

Among the ways an organisation can develop higher harmony are-

- between itself and the customer
- among the people in the firm
- among the parts or components of the organisation (job
- positions, activities, systems, projects, etc.)
- between the advocacy of high business values and their implementation in the details of the organisation

When an organisation operates with each part pulling in its own direction, disharmony ensues, creating a sort of group ego. However, when the organisation recognises this disharmony and makes efforts to organise, coordinate, and integrate its parts, creating a sense of harmony among them, remarkable outcomes can occur. A prime example illustrating this power of harmony in business is the story of Chrysler under the leadership of Lee Iacocca. Through greater coordination and integration of its components, Chrysler swiftly became the most profitable company in the car industry. By enabling all parts to work efficiently and in unison, Chrysler established a level of harmony that facilitated one of the greatest turnarounds in corporate history.

Connecting with life and others

The question is then how we can achieve a state of consciousness that would allow us to be more connected and One with life around us.

The answer lies in connecting to our inner and living from the deeper parts of our being rather than remaining on the surface of life. By connecting to our inner, greater will be our affinity, connection, and harmony with our surroundings, including the people we interact with.

But how do we reach that silent state, that witness consciousness that would enable us to feel more connected with the world and others? We can start building this new inner state by continuously opening ourselves to the spiritual Force. By dedicating and consecrating our upcoming activities to a Higher Power, not only conditions of life quickly set right, but we develop an ever-wider opening to our deeper Self. As we become familiar with these profound Silent and Still parts within, we experience a growing bond with the world around us, including the situations we encounter and the people we interact with. These harmonic experiences not only generate immense power for success but deep inner joy and fulfillment. In the atmosphere of harmony, one cannot help but be taken to the stars!

Given this perspective, consider asking yourself: In what areas of my life can I create greater harmony? Identifying these areas and making sincere efforts to bring harmony, you will not only generate a vast power for accomplishment, but you will experience deep, inner fulfillment, as the separation between yourself and life will melt into blissful Oneness.

Contradictions are Complements-Resolving through Higher Harmony

Life's Character: Progress Through Contradiction

Life has a character, just like we humans. Life expresses itself through a number of laws, overt or subtle principles. One such principle is that progress occurs through contradiction and conflict with others and circumstances. It is only through these contradicting relationships that each party can make a breakthrough in consciousness and thereby progress. Finding higher harmony beyond the contradiction allows each side to move forward, while failure to do so leads to stagnation or regression. This dynamic is pervasive, evident in both personal lives and the world at large, representing Nature's secret method. A closely related principle is that the greater the opposition we face in life, the greater the opportunity for us to rise and grow.

Nature's method of evolution-Contradictions

In lower consciousness, we perceive division, contradictions, opposition, conflict everywhere. Life is viewed through a lens of contradictions: pleasure versus pain, good versus bad, positive versus negative, my rights versus yours, spirit versus matter, and so forth. In higher consciousness, however, these dualities are seen not as contradictions but as complements. For instance, a man's conflict with his neighbour is a mechanism for the evolution of both parties. The "conflict" serves as Nature's way of lifting the consciousness of both sides and facilitating broader progress for the world and the Creation. This is the evolutionary aim of Nature. In this perspective, evil can be seen as just a great, if not greater, spur than the normal "good" to enable the true Good to increase. Thus, good and evil work together to foster progress and evolution, functioning as complements rather than contradictions as perceived by our lower, surface consciousness.

Nature vs. Soul's Method of Progress

When the Manifest emerged from the Unmanifest through the deliberate action of the latter, Life divided into two aspects: Nature and Soul (known in Indian terms as Prakriti and Purusha). **Nature** represents **Life's slow and challenging path**, which is the typical way humans experience the world. **Soul, or Spirit**, embodies Life's method of **progress through higher consciousness**, producing only positive effects without any negative. (I.e. it is Self-existent.)

Man is dominated by Nature, evolving slowly and painfully through division, duality, and the interplay of pleasure and pain. However, he has the potential to evolve through Soul or Spirit instead, progressing rapidly with no negative outcomes. Nature's challenging path was sanctioned by the Divine to allow for the greatest multiplicity of forms, forces, and aspects in creation, facilitating the widest variety of Rich Delight. When we move from Nature to Soul by discovering our highest nature, we experience the Rich Delight for which life was created. The Divine intended to extend its static Delight into dynamic Delight through the self-discovery of forms of Creation – i.e. we – fulfilling the intent of the Infinite.

Nature's vs. Self-Directed Tapas

The Sanskrit word "Tapas" means "spiritual discipline." For **a yogi**, this might involve prolonged meditation to connect with the Spirit. For **someone committed to personal growth**, it might mean learning to remain calm in the face of an abusive boss or short-tempered spouse.

In both instances, the aim is to achieve an evolution of consciousness through **inner discipline**.

Above two inner disciplines are consciously self-embraced. However there is a third one, which is the normal way of life and imposed by life. It is the tapas that **life imposes on us**. This is Nature compelling us to adopt certain inner or outer strategies to overcome limitations and achieve personal progress.

In that way, each of us are compelled by Nature to move forward in consciousness; whether it means standing up to an abusive partner; or being a more understanding manager, when one is not normally disposed that way; or being forced to do things we are reluctant to do. It is the Tapas of Nature forced on us, secretly working in our own best interest, so we can overcome personal limitations, enabling us to grow in consciousness. In Jane Austen's "Pride and Prejudice," Mr. Bennet, the father of five daughters, is forced into the discipline of not reacting to his vulgar, loud-mouthed, wife. This tapas serves as a means for his personal development.

In a similar manner, each of us is pushed by Nature to advance in consciousness. This might involve standing up to an abusive partner, becoming a more understanding manager despite our natural tendencies, or being forced to undertake tasks we are unwilling to do. It is the Tapas of Nature, imposed upon us, secretly working in our best interest to help us overcome personal limitations and grow in consciousness.

Conscious Tapas or Evolution

While embracing the Tapas required by Nature is beneficial, consciously directing our lives through self-discipline is even more advantageous. Conscious Tapas can be practiced at two levels:

1. **Discipline for fulfillment in life:** This includes developing knowledge and skills, improving personal organisation, building psychological strength, and eliminating negative attitudes.

2. **Discipline for fulfillment in spirit:**   This involves turning awareness inward, practicing non-reaction and stillness, opening to spiritual forces, meditating deeply, and praying. By engaging in conscious, self-directed tapas or discipline, we evolve our consciousness, lead more successful and fulfilling lives, and attract good fortune, making it superior to merely following Nature's imposed Tapas.

Perceiving Dualities: Lower vs. Higher Consciousness

In lower consciousness, we see division and conflict. We see life as a struggle filled with contradictions and conflicts. We view it as a series of contradictions: pleasure versus pain, good versus bad, positive versus negative, and more. However, in higher consciousness, these dual pairs are perceived not as contradictions, but as complements.

For instance, a man's conflict with his neighbor is a mechanism for the evolution of both parties. The "conflict" serves as Nature's way of lifting the consciousness of both sides and facilitating broader progress for the world.

In that light, evil can be recognised as just as powerful, if not greater a spur as the normal "good" to enable the true Good to increase. Good and evil thus work together to spur progress and evolution, functioning as complements rather than contradictions as perceived by our lower, surface consciousness.

On the surface, all we see is contradiction, but from a deeper perspective, we see each conflicting party represents complementary aspects evolving through their interactions. Thus, contradictions are truly complements.

Moving Beyond Contradiction and Progress through Resolution of Contradiction

Life evolves or can evolve through the contradictions of two parties, whether spouse or family members, associates, organisations, nations, etc.

Life and Nature thus establishes and urges the further evolution of each side of the contradiction. Without conflict and the subsequent attempts at resolution, would remain static, or even fall back.

When immersed in such contradictions, our aim should be to seek higher harmony for resolution, facilitating further progress. This often entails rising in consciousness to discover a higher Centre of being. This can involve shedding a corresponding negative attitude, by withdrawing a wanting emotion, by giving up a stale habit, developing new understandings, transcending ego, bridging divides, moving beyond selfishness, adopting new approaches to life, or adjusting values and beliefs.

In each circumstance, understanding the contradiction as well as what is required to resolve it and the steps needed for resolution is crucial. Both sides of the conflict must contradiction need to take that approach for optimal results and collective progress. By making inner and outer efforts toward resolution, life often responds positively from unexpected sources.

In essence, through our inner and outer endeavors to engage a higher Centre of being, we resolve conflicts, ushering in higher harmony and enabling new levels of progress.

Resolving Contradictions through Higher Harmony: Husband Vs Wife Interactions

From our surface view, we tend to express our ego, defending our own position in a conflict. However, Nature suggests that our adversary or conflicting partner is actually our complement. For instance, a man has the quality of feeling that he is not being listened to by others, particularly his wife, who tends to be absorbed in her own activities and doesn't listen when he speaks. This leads to irritation for him. To resolve this, the man must evolve out of his insecurity, while the woman must overcome her unresponsiveness for her evolution. The evolution of both of them can only occur through their interaction. Life has brought them together to serve this evolutionary purpose. It is only through the interaction with the other person that one's own faults show themselves. Thus _the conflicting person is an agent for our own personal growth_. The same principle is applicable not only at home, but in all other areas of our life, whether it be the workplace, society, etc.

Thus life evolves through contradictions of two parties, through these conflicting pairs. Our objective should be to recognise these contradictions and transcend them by overcoming corresponding limitations within ourselves. In doing so, we progress and grow, often invoking sudden good fortune. Complete knowledge is incapable of selfishness, domination or evil. Nature awaits our progress, evolution, and transformation. But we have to take the first decisive step. It is to recognise the contradiction as a beneficial complement that is key to our personal growth.

Perception Shift: From Contradiction to Harmony

The reason we primarily perceive division and contradiction in our relationships, rather than recognising their complementary nature, is due to the limitations of our minds. Mind depieces. Mind cannot see the whole truth of any subject, inquiry, or matter, but only the part. When engaged in conflict, our minds only perceive the conflict, which is only a part of a much wider truth, and wholeness of possibilities. Moreover, they tend to prioritise satisfying the ego's interests, disregarding the greater good. As one moves out of this partial view into the whole truth of any situation – conflicting or not – then one begins to perceive the full integral knowledge of the conditions of life in any moment with a sense of marvel. By transcending ego, we gain new perspective, new solutions emerge, The limited, finite world steeped in conflict will burst forth with infinite possibilities coming from this new harmonic perspective. We will then together with our once-adversarial partner stand before entirely new possibilities for progress and accomplishment. That discovery will in turn itself release a deep abiding joy within.

Outer Surface Mind is Inversion of Inner Subliminal Mind

The human mind is a curious thing. What we see on the surface, our outer thoughts and feelings, can be quite different from what lies in our inner. This deeper layer, called the subliminal mind, holds our true evolutionary aspirations. It's often said that we're drawn to things that our conscious selves might dislike or find distasteful – a hint that something deeper is at play. The human mind is constructed in a way that one's surface mind is exactly the reverse of one's wider, deeper, truer Mind, the subliminal. All happenings in our life are the invitations from our subconscious and subliminal.

Age and experience can bring a sense of calmness, which is often mistaken for a loss of FIRE. Marriage helps the fire to die down. Maturity is mistaken as a loss of warmth in personality. The human mind is structured in such a way that its surface perspective often opposes the deeper, truer subliminal mind. Consequently, a person is often driven by their subliminal mind to pursue what their surface mind detests or finds repulsive. This dynamic frequently plays out in employment and even more so in marriage. To know that our Surface Mind is inversely moved by the deep-seated subliminal that knows the entire universe is the very first spiritual realisation.

An incessant talker is often drawn to a silent spouse, and a miserly man may seek a spendthrift wife. This creates an ongoing divergence in their aspirations. Others might console them with the saying, "marriages are made in heaven." At a ripe old age, such couples often realise that their marital experiences was a rewarding one as each was complementary to the other.

The trait that has long caused you the problem for a long time, is the door that can open upon progress, such as rough speech, assertion, or impatience. Conversely, the trait that has consistently served you can now take you further very fast to the end, e.g. soft speech, goodwill, integrity, reliability, etc.

HUMAN NATURE SEEKS INTENSITY through SPIRIT OF CONTRADICTION

Human nature instinctively operates in a spirit of contradiction, as the intensity needed for action arises from opposites. By contradicting and opposing others, we indirectly gain the knowledge. Our lack of energy for receiving direct knowledge and insights from life is compensated by responding in a contradictory manner. Due to our contradicting behaviour and acts, we attract outer embarrassment. Outer embarrassment is the outcome of our inner perversion. It is the way of human nature to seek harmony through quarrel, conflict. Conflict, opposition, contradiction loses its intensity by gathering knowledge through reconciliation and matures into mutuality and harmony. It is the way of evolution of our perceptions and wisdom.

Whatever our Being inherently knows, those truths are perceived inversely by our outer surface mind. Life is shaped by our being, not by our mind. Self-awareness comes from reconciliation of contradictions within oneself. Once mental confusions are resolved, problems vanish. Reconciliation on the outside is made possible by our inner realisation. Realisation comes by participation through observation. We should have a perceptive mind and consciousness to gain wisdom from the happenings of our life and life around us.

Unconscious to Conscious Evolution

Contradictions is the method adopted by Nature for its evolution. Man in his inner is always unconsciously seeking self expression and self exprcrience for his evolution. Man initially seeks power, later knowledge. Man can collaborate in his own evolution. Man can shift from unconscious evolution to conscious evolution to abridge the time of his self- evolution. Humans have an intense capacity to change in moments.

To be able to scc that outer is coming from inner is the ultimate Supramental Janana(Wisdom). It is wise to observe that whatever advice we give to others is equally applicable to ourselves at that point of time in our life. This is the design of life. To understand is wisdom. The true function of mind is to understand without thoughts. Behind the magic of the finite, there is the logic of the infinite. What we know by thoughts, should be known by our feelings but it takes several years. Man is more awake at mental level than his emotional and physical level. Even if man remains unconscious, his life experiences keep accumulating at psychic level and evolution happens to man unconsciously.

The Lord delights in the evolution of His creation. When our perception changes, our problem dissolves. When physical sensitivity changes, it brings transformation both ways, in the inner and outer. When the mind understands this transformation, our problems will turn out as opportunities. If man seeks outside a particular thing, life grips our neck as intolerable problem in all its intensity. If the vision is turned inwards, life embraces us as a Marvel.

Evolution at various levels

Humility: Brings the evolution of the body.

Worship: Brings the evolution of emotions.

Faith: Brings the evolution of the mind.

Brahma Janam(Wisdom):   Brings the evolution of the soul.

Consecration: Brings the evolution of the inner psychic Spirit

Few examples of Complementaries in the World

1.   Silence and Speech are complementary. Like so, all aspects in Creation.

2.   Obstacles are opportunities.

3.   Hate is love.

4.   Failure is potential success.

5.   Manifestation is limited Absolute.

6.   Pain is a concealed delight.

7. Ignorance is a concealed knowledge.

8. Negative is a concealed positive.

9. Obstacle is a concealed opportunity.

10. Every error is a possibility of discovery of truth.

11. Every failure and weakness is a first sounding of the gulf of the power of potentials inside.

12. All strength and success lie in wait, concealed inside the apparent manifesting weakness and failure.

13. Dark is intense light.

14. White is all colors reflected. Black is all colors absorbed.

15. Failure is intense success.

16. Finite is intense infinite.

17. Poverty is intense Prosperity

18. Undivine is intense Divine

19. Matter is intense Spirit.

20. Contradiction is intense complement.

21. Evil is intense good.

22. Evolution is intense involution.

23. Inconscient is intense superconscient.

Pain and Suffering: Gateways to Evolution

All disease is a means towards some new joy of health, all evil & pain a turning of Nature for some more intense bliss & good, all death an opening on widest immortality, why and how this should be so, is God's secret which only the soul purified of egoism can penetrate. Our suffering and pain in surface consciousness is due to our character and attitude, EGO. But there is an evolutionary reason behind pain and suffering. Pain expands us. Pain helps us to come out of our limitations TO EVOLVE AND GROW. PAIN HAS SECRET WIDENING POWER.

War is the father of all things. Evolution progresses in apparent contradictions beneath which there is a harmonic whole and inherent unity. To realise the inherent unity and all bliss in the creation is the evolutionary aim. The enjoyment of unity in division is richer than the enjoyment of standalone unity. Hence the Supreme Absolute has created this Existence to Delight and enjoy its Unity in Existence by multiplying itself.

In the Universe,

- Ignorance is apparent. But knowledge is inherent.
- Division is apparent. But Unity is inherent.
- Supermind is aware of the inherent unity.

From evolutionary point of view,

- Ignorance is the starting point of Knowledge.
- Imperfection is the starting point of Perfection.

Unfulfillment is the starting point of Fulfillment.

This CREATION is really not a creation but BECOMING of the SUPREME BEING.

Gold Vessel is really not just a vessel but still gold. Gold vessel is becoming of the Gold. This CREATION is really not a Creation other than the Creator, Supreme Being but BECOMING of the SUPREME BEING. This Creation is Supreme Being, Supreme Spirit. This Creation is made out of the substance of Spirit and Spirit's Light. Spirit became Matter through Involution. Through Evolution, now Matter has to manifest the buried Spirit and become Spirit. Matter is Spirit. The contradictions of what we see as Matter and Spirit, Science and Spirituality are not contradictions but complements.

Strength, Simplicity, Grace, Evolutionary Aspiration for surface of the Psychic Soul

Strength comes by birth or by experience. Simplicity and strength are the same. Simplicity and strength is Brahman and Spirit. Realising this one can acquire strength. Aspiration rises for transformation when we get rid of all habits.

For those on the path of yoga, grounding oneself in the soul is essential. To recognise grace, is gratitude. To see life in lifeless action, gives life to the action. To see grace in adverse circumstances, makes the grace as supergrace. The soul can recognise grace. The soul which comes to the surface while recognising the grace is the psychic soul. One's evolutionary aspiration makes the psychic soul to surface. Psychic soul sees all life's happenings from the point of highest harmony as it is in constant touch with the Superconscient Spirit.

Contradictions and Oppositions are our Evolutionary Awakeners

Universe makes us evolve by bringing contradicting situations and persons in our life. Till we overcome the situation or person by our inner transformation, universe keeps on sending such contradictions, oppositions in different forms pushing us to learn, completely transform us and outgrow the need for such contradictions.

They are our awakeners. Such contradictions and oppositions force us to go to our inner depths and bring out our potential. Whoever is opposing or challenging us is really bringing GRACE to us.

85

Developing Complementarity in intensifying relationships

The whole secret of life lies in the unity of opposites and the complementarity of contradictions, which form the spiritual essence of any relationship. When we fully embrace and accept the current conditions of life, sudden good fortune will come our way. When we focus on the interests and concerns of others, not only do we develop more cordial and harmonious relationships but life often moves on our behalf with astonishing results.

First, we must examine the negative side—specifically, the troubling relationships we have with others. Before we can consider the best ways to connect with people, we must shed our harmful feelings and emotions toward them. And yet even efforts to dissolve the negative, will attract the powerful life response.

Reversing the inner negative feelings : A Woman's Journey to Full-Time Employment

A woman who had been a temporary employee for ten years harbored jealousy and harsh feelings towards her permanent co-workers. One day she attended a seminar on taking control of one's life, which focused on developing and implementing a 30-day improvement plan. Inspired, she decided to use this approach to pursue her goal of obtaining a permanent, full-time job. She shared her efforts with her friend. Initially, her progress seemed promising, but when she discussed it further, her friend, a life

94

response practitioner, noticed that something was wrong in the way she described her relationships with her co-workers. She admitted about her feeling of a certain amount of animosity toward several of her co-workers. Her friend gently raised the issue by empathising with her, finally came straight out and said that even the best-laid plans to secure a permanent position would fail if her venomous feelings and emotions persisted. Then she was advised by her friend to let go of all negative feelings toward them if she wanted any chance of attracting a full-time position.

After grappling with these harsh truths, she finally saw the light. Though it was not an easy road over the next several weeks, she made a sincere effort to change her negative attitudes toward her coworkers. In fact, at one point, she not only established cordial relationship with several of them, but actually began to be friendly with one or two! As it turned out, when her psychological effort reached its peak, she received a most unexpected call from her manager, offering her a promotion to a full-time position, citing her exemplary work.

After absorbing the initial shock, she began to question how this could have happened. She soon realised that this sudden and unexpected change in fortune was due to her sincere psychological effort to overcome her negative attitudes and feelings. When that effort reached its peak, she released a concentration of positive energy that attracted the magnificent response, ending years of frustration and failure.

When we make the effort to bridge the psychological gap between us, life responds in our favour.

Positive ways to connect with people

The most fundamental way to establish positive and bonding relationships is to shift our focus away from ourselves and towards the interests and concerns of others, embracing their point of view, giving others greater personal attention, etc. Each trait has the power to evoke the miraculous.

That is because they are movements away from our limited, separate selves to a wider, universal field. It is in essence a shift away from ego and self absorption to a higher state of **selfless and self-giving behaviour**. To be selfless means avoiding focusing on oneself in relation to others, expressing humility and modesty. On the other hand, being self-giving goes a step further, extending ourselves for the benefit of others without expecting anything in return. Though they differ slightly, they share the common outcome that when practiced more, life quickly responds.

Close relationships turning into ill-will

Even when we have very positive relationships with others, a closer and more intense relationship can sometimes turn into ill-will.

All life progresses through contradictions, or rather their resolution into higher harmony. When we come into closer contact with others, our contradictory nature with them is accentuated. General contradictions turn into very specific contradictions. One's negative rubs with your negative, and this dynamic intensifies in closer relationships. The relationship which started as a bonding and alloying one, gradually breaks and turn into disgusting one. The one which started with goodwill turned into ill-will.

However, such intensities of contradiction offer perfect opportunities for their resolution. From our side, we can find the wanting correspondence, and make the change. Whether the other person in that particular challenging situation wishes to raise his consciousness in that particular challenging situation is for them to decide.

It is often said that every outer condition is a reflection of one's inner state. Similarly, every outer situation is an opportunity for our progress. Indeed, these situations provide the right conditions to enable that best and fastest progress if we are attentive and proactive in responding to them.

As we grow closer to others, we have the opportunity to deepen our connection, leading to not only the avoidance of negative contradictions but also the maintenance of joyful and even blissful interactions. However, a common challenge is failing to allocate time for creating **"mental space"** for examining relationships as they intensify through closer quarters and relations.

We just get sucked into it without ongoing reflection and self-evaluation of conditions. Creating a quieter, deeper internal space can greatly aid in navigating these intensifying personal relationships.

Such situations are apt to practice Non-reaction, and Taking the Other Person's perspective. In fact, with such intensity, we can become their Masters. Ultimately, the goal is harmony—a higher harmony born out of resolving contradictions and one that can be fostered by the force of universal and spiritual energy.

When we attain the consciousness of the Absolute, of supramental perception, conflicts cease to appear as contradictions but rather as complements, as it affords the best opportunity for our fastest, richest, and most perfect growth. This realisation is for those who have seriously taken to a life of Conscious Evolution (Yoga).

Suggestions for Harmonious, Intimate Relations

Here are few suggestions for better, more harmonious and more intimate relations:

- Avoid criticising.
- Refrain from complaining, blaming.
- Respond without negativity.
- Avoid trying to one-up the other person.
- Refrain from imposing your will, assertion.
- Avoid trying to change the other person.

- Offer compliments on small things.
- Give without expecting anything in return.
- Strive to raise the level of harmony.
- Treat your partner as you would an honored guest. Give them their own space and freedom.

These are the life-equations. Having knowledge of these equations and wisely applying in one's life will help in a great way to attract powerful life conditions. Rather than worrying or despairing over breaking relationships, one has the freedom to shift their perspectives about oneself, others, situations and navigate life's ups and downs by inner work and inner reversal of consciousness.

Influence of parents' consciousness on children -Intensifying the relationships

When we focus our mental energy on a particular concept and make efforts to delve deeper into it, those close to us, such as our children, often gain knowledge of it directly, even without discussing it with them. This happens at the inner level. Parents and children are connected psychologically in inner planes of Existence and as the parents raise in their consciousness, it subliminally influences and helps the children to rise too.

For instance, while I was writing this book on inner work and life response, absorbed in the stream of organising my thoughts for expression through writing, I had not discussed anything with my daughter. One day, surprisingly my daughter came and told me that many of her friends were approaching her and seeking guidance for how to overcome the inner challenges they face within mentally and emotionally and how to bring the inner transformation within. And when I asked her what reply she gave to her friends about certain inner challenges, the answer she gave was exactly the process which I was writing at that time. What I was focusing and organising in my consciousness was the knowledge she got directly without my outer expression. This is the power of inner organisation and life response. Many times I have seen that the insights shared by my daughter to me about certain life responses are exactly the same concepts and processes which my consciousness was absorbed in during that time.

One tip for parents who truly want their children to grow, evolve and accomplish. Many times we are constrained to interact with our children due to several reasons. The constraints may be in the form of time, less physical proximity (children may be far away), limitation in the understanding of children about concern of the parents towards them for their well- being, etc. However, there is a way for parents to silently contribute to their children's growth and well-being. It is an inner work which parents can do anywhere, anytime irrespective of wherever the children may be. If parents inwardly organise and raise their consciousness and personality, invoke their inner spirit and deeply aspire for the well-being of their children and keep on intensifying it day by day, they can see it manifest in the lives of their children. Children inherit their parents' physical and psychological traits. The traits of the parents show up in the behaviour of children. The being of the parents and children are wired together in the subliminal inner mind which is behind and deeper than our surface physical mind. Parents by reversing their inner and raising in consciousness and in silence aspire for children to evolve, will have a more profound effect on the inner being of the children and their growth. This is one of the most effective ways of intensifying the relationships.

86

Atmosphere

By atmosphere we mean one's inner atmosphere and outer atmosphere of life. Both play a very important role in the process of any accomplishment or manifestation in life. Inner atmosphere influences the outer atmosphere and outer influences the inner. We need a great deal of patience and a very wide and integral vision to comprehend how things work in life. Atmosphere can be seen in different dimensions and perspectives.

Various Effects of Atmosphere on Success

1. At the beginning of a meeting with someone, making an effort to focus on their needs and concerns, setting aside your own will create the best atmosphere for attracting a successful outcome.

2. In a positive atmosphere, negatives are eventually absorbed by the positive, whereas in a negative atmosphere, the opposite occurs. For example, a man makes a foolish mistake in a conference, but because the conference is enveloped in a positive atmosphere, it will turn out very successful, and even his mistake turns into an advantage.

3. In an **atmosphere of humility** and eager interest in others, unexpected positive conditions, solutions, and opportunities present themselves.

4. **Effect of Soft Speech on Atmosphere**: Practicing "soft speech" by speaking in a low, gentle voice can create an atmosphere of calm, which attracts the best conditions. For example, a 39-year-old wealthy American businessperson faced the loss of all 60 employees and was

on the brink of bankruptcy. However, following a relative's suggestion, he and others in the organisation began speaking in a softer, quiet voice. As a result, within two years, the owner was in a financial position to retire for life.

5. A child of seven learns more effectively on their own in an encouraging, free atmosphere than a twelve-year-old does under the current system of education. It is a fact.

6. The **land or house**, even an apparent physical thing carries the atmosphere and spirit of the house or land owner. It has the power to influence the work and lives of the workers. The house or land of a spiritual person carries their vibrations and casts a positive influence.

7. Consider a family where the atmosphere is quarrelsome. If they teach themselves to view issues from another person's perspective, all quarrels will suddenly vanish. When the spirit is awake, it can easily see the other man's point of view.

8. **Domestic atmosphere** rises drastically when the relationship between husband and wife is harmonious and each one wishes for the well-being of other. When husband truly listens to wife or vice versa, this mutuality has profound power to make the atmosphere at home POSITIVE in the very best sense of the word.

9. **Atmosphere of Self Giving**:- When someone tries to deprive you of something, they activate the key of Self-giving in the atmosphere. As a result, the atmosphere responds by providing you with that same thing in greater measure, transforming the negative intention into a positive outcome. If you see anyone's life with this insight, you can see numerous examples. Even in films, novels we come across such instances. There is a logic behind the life force or the mechanism through which this force operates.

2 examples

1. A business competitor attempts to sabotage another company by spreading false rumors. Instead of causing harm, the targeted company receives an outpouring of support from customers

and partners who rally against the unfair treatment, resulting in increased business and a stronger reputation.

2. In a family, parents may show favouritism towards one child over their siblings. For instance, parents might consistently praise and support the academic achievements of their eldest child while neglecting or undervaluing the efforts and accomplishments of their younger children. Later what has been deprived for younger children will be given by life abundantly through someone.

10. The **ill-will directed** towards one person generally results in another person experiencing goodwill. When one invokes the Spirit, they are surrounded by an atmosphere of goodwill, which inherently can only bring about positive outcomes. For instance, if your boss becomes angry and desires to punish you, the atmosphere surrounding you is activated, but it can only produce positive effects. Thus, the punishment your boss intends to inflict can unexpectedly turn into a beneficial outcome, such as receiving a gift. In an example, a mean boss deprives a subordinate of using the office cycle to commute, a facility he had enjoyed for a long time. However, the subordinate's neighbor offers to transport him on their motorbike, and other colleagues also offer assistance. In ordinary life, this does happen, but not often. But for those who invoke the spirit, it becomes a permanent feature. It will be a rich yogic knowledge if one is patient to SEE how the spiritual force and life works. By invocation of spirit the evil atmosphere changes to good.

11. In our life situation, **the presence or absence of a person is not a random chance** but a conscious design of the creator and has got great significance. When we are discussing a subject, a person's arrival in the scene indicates the person's interest in the subject. This is irrespective of the fact whether the person has connection with the subject or not. The very fact of discussion attracts the person on the scene.

12. We always carry within ourselves the **atmosphere of** our **acts**.

Atmosphere Of Spirit

When the Spirit is evoked the atmosphere changes. A life of utter Truthfulness brings one into the atmosphere of Spirit. When one's inner spirit emerges on the surface, life expands, work flowers and creates an atmosphere of harmony and progress.

For someone who has taken to invoking the Spirit, life will be one of marvellous unfolding. Life changes, and the very atmosphere of family is transformed. Suddenly, children appear to express affection more readily. The boss who usually frowns, suddenly smiles. Even a wife, after a prolonged period of emotional distance or a long break of dry years becomes more intimate, openly acknowledging your value and reviving the earlier romance. It feels as though one is riding high on waves of psychological admiration. In this way, the Spirit gives what the surface being was unsuccessfully craving for all these days and years.

A national spiritual atmosphere comes into existence when all parts or most of the parts of a nation awaken to the spirit of the nation. In such an atmosphere, Poverty recedes and Prosperity flourishes.

Spirit gives us deeper insights and intuition

The Spirit's atmosphere helps us see things others might miss. When five people have been searching for a lost object for some time in vain, your calm mind will give the capacity to suddenly spot it. It is the insight of vision. Insight generally comes as a thought, but can arise through any of the senses. Yet, intuition is even stronger than insight. Insight is like a door that opens on Intuition, which gives us even deeper understanding and guidance.

Spiritual atmosphere in WORK

- It is often seen as a mother's duty to make sure her child sits down and does their homework. It is equivalent to punishment. But there are schools that don't give homework. Instead, they focus on helping kids learn early, reading at the age of 4 or even 3. In such cases, a child might wake up and take a book and start reading. All day long that child is found reading. The parent's role then is to continue to supply books. This idea extends beyond education. If we teach workers the right skill of doing their work, they might not go home until their work is perfectly done.

- In a school where memorisation was prioritised over creative writing, compositions became a tedious task, but when students were taught to write English, their enthusiasm for writing blossomed, changing the whole atmosphere. Each student was anxious to write and started summarising retold stories. Most of them did so for ten or fifteen books which exceeded the expectations unimaginably. Work has a spirit in it. To evoke that will give great results.

- Management often believes in authority. Exercise of authority does work. But there is an alternative method, which is better. To release the enthusiasm of the worker. Then authority will be superfluous. Then to train the enthusiasm into a skill. In that case, no supervision will be necessary at all. Each will be conscious of his own skill. In such an atmosphere it is not easy to make the worker leave the factory at the closing hour. In England during the Second World War, there were instances where workers arrived for their shifts half an hour early and were unwilling to leave when their shifts were over. It is the authority of work which is far better than the authority of the management. Greater than the authority of work is the Spirit of the work. Spirit released in any work does not fail to bring exceeding results.

Spirit's Equilibrium

Equilibrium is of the Spirit. **One's atmosphere should maintain equilibrium.** When equilibrium is disturbed, problem arises. Once we regain our equilibrium, our understanding becomes complete. Then the problem leaves us.

Nothing works when the atmosphere is not ready or ripe. In an atmosphere where opportunities sail in, problems find no soil to strike roots.

By becoming as vast as the universe one can find real repose. Instead of endlessly unfolding thoughts, one can attempt to get into a state of silence. Getting into silence is a higher accomplishment. It is wise to know the science of life, the functioning of life, how life responds in accordance with our inner consciousness.

In yoga one realises that over 75%, of physical ailments are due to ill-will from others, grace coming in that is blocked inside, personal reluctance or unwillingness, breakdown of one's psychological balance, general negative atmosphere, nerves overwrought, breakdown in material conditions such as lack of funds, resistance of the physical consciousness to grow further, etc. Outer conditions just reflect that. The Mother says that the physical illnesses due to material, biological illnesses are less than 10%.

There is an inner work to do for transformation. The salvation is in life and not in death. The only thing that never fails is the Supreme Truth. Transformation of consciousness is followed by transformation of the body, which is of physical substance. For the transformation of the body, one has to discover the supreme reality and spirit in the centre of the body's cells and atoms. Equilibrium is the basis for all transformations. Spirit has to be on the surface constantly for profound transformations.

Spiritual energy

Spiritual energy is superior to vital or mental energy. Just as replacing an oil lamp with an electric lantern enhances illumination, substituting mental energy with spiritual energy in work yields greater results. A spiritual atmosphere achieves more through its silent influence compared to a mental atmosphere. Consider the impact of having the CEO oversee a shipment instead of a floor supervisor—productivity increases significantly. Similarly, when reading, one can prioritising spiritual intelligence over mental intelligence. Then we read faster, understand better and are able to convey information more effectively.

Spiritual intelligence

Invoking the spirit has the power to achieve the seemingly impossible. Those who make this invocation a guiding principle in their lives will gradually find themselves immersed in the atmosphere of the Spirit. As a university of intellectual climate releases one's mental intelligence, a spiritual atmosphere releases spiritual intelligence within us. This spiritual intelligence allows us to recognise and utilise subtle opportunities and luck in our lives.

Living in The Atmosphere of Spirit

Seventy years ago, a spiritual seeker wrote, "Aspiration awakes in me, achieve in me all that I flame for," In that piece of writing he also says, "You have given me more than what I ignorantly asked for." The Spirit never gives what we ask for, but always gives more.

Once a woman, well-employed, came into this atmosphere, took to the invocation of spirit seriously, and saw that surprises in life are ever present. Despite facing challenges, she quickly realised the significance of remaining in Spirit's atmosphere and resolved NOT to move out of the atmosphere whose novelty and creativity was a standing wonder to her. The company where she worked introduced a voluntary retirement plan, offering full salary to employees over fifty until the end of their service. When we are in the atmosphere of the Spirit, things happen like this. To us, it is a surprise and we accept it with pleasure and gratitude.

To the Spirit, it is the only way it knows how to act in our lives. It is the Spirit's way of giving. Spirit pours, not trickles. It is the characteristic of Infinity.

Perceiving Subtle signs of Life

When we become aware of life's subtle workings and principles beyond mere mechanical workings, we will see how life truly operates, including the phenomena of life response. We will perceive that the world is subtly organised through interconnected forces and energies across space and time because all existence has a Spiritual source where everything begins in integral unity. This profound oneness continues in the life plane and can be truly perceived, experienced, and understood, when we rise to our higher and deepest consciousness.

There is an outer priority of things one is compelled to follow. However, there is a deeper, more subtle inner priority that, when recognised, aligns one with the higher intentions and flow of life. By following this inner guidance carefully and spontaneously, one experiences an existence of perpetual miraculousness.

All around us are Subtle signs indicating the current plans for our future, both positive and negative. Recognising these signs equips us to discern what to do and what to avoid, facilitating optimal outcomes in our lives. Observing and watching life closely, we know that life is always suggesting what to embrace and what to avoid. Separating our desires and needs from these observations, keeping out the ego, being objective and neutral, we can perceive the subtle signs of life to guide our decisions, actions and life.

Every Act Is Announced Beforehand

The idea that every action or event in the world is preceded by a prior act is a constant phenomenon in the universe. However, this is often too subtle for the average person to perceive. By developing our consciousness to a higher level, we can increasingly observe this marvel of life in action.

How can this benefit us? If life is constantly signaling what is to come and when we have that knowledge, then we gain a significant advantage in navigating the Game of Life.

Overhead Signage and food quality

During a break from his training work, Ray was about to place an order at a restaurant when he noticed that the item he wanted wasn't visible on the overhead signage. He pointed this out to the order taker, who then made it available. However, when Ray ordered from that part of the signage, the food turned out to be overcooked and unsatisfying.

What's the lesson here? The initial problem with the signage was a sign of the poor quality of the food to come. Recognising such associations can be incredibly useful. When we become aware of these signs, we can offer the problem—in this case, the incorrect signage—to the spiritual force so that it would cancel the negative which comes in the form of poor food.

In essence, whenever we notice a negative unfolding, it's beneficial to consecrate it or take other precautions, depending on the situation. This way, we can avoid many negative circumstance that are indicated beforehand and are likely to come our way.

Certain other signs

- Rejecting others can be seen as a fortunate act because it the rejection of the misfortune that comes through them. It shields us from the misfortune they may bring into our lives. Life acts through us and makes us reject.

- Our words sometimes inadvertently disclose our underlying motives, bringing them to our awareness. The words voiced may come from our subconscious contrary to our outer awareness which carries deeper truths of things.

- A conscious effort to hide our defects leads to exposing them unconsciously.

- Unexpectedness often stems from unconsciousness.

- To learn a thing, we often tend to express its opposite.

Perceiving Subtle Signs And Managing Expectations In Relationships

M cherished spending time with his elder brother, finding their interactions valuable. While the elder brother also enjoyed their time together, but often it was to oblige the younger that he visited him. They met frequently, but not as often as the younger one desired, who wished for daily visits. The younger sibling was enthusiastic, while the elder was courteous, though unaware of the younger one's longing. The younger could not know that his insistence would postpone the meeting. On the third day, the younger kept his morning free of engagements so that the elder's visit would not be interfered with. There was no sign of the elder brother or any message of his coming. The younger brother asked another person to find out what had happened. The reply came that the elder brother was occupied for several days. Had the younger brother perceived the subtle sign of life relating to this elder brother's continuous absence and correlated to his inner insistence, over-expectation which created loss of life's equilibrium and balance and trained his MIND not to expect by bringing equality in him, the elder brother would have been anxious to see him every day.

Accomplish by flowing with life

In our heightened state of consciousness, we recognise this flow in all its wonder. Conversely, in moments of lower awareness, we miss the subtle perceptions and the miracles.

If a computer operating system requires an online upgrade, our initial reaction may be resistance and frustration as it disrupts our familiar routine. However, when we approach the situation with a mindful and sensitive mindset, we recognise its need, letting go of our distress, and take up the necessary activities and actions that life is now pointing to. Then when we return to the fresh, new things that had to unfold, we see how necessary it was in the broader context of life.

Moreover, each alternative task we engage in during the upgrade process, such as cleaning the kitchen, can yield valuable outcomes. It may even lead to unexpected strokes of good fortune; for instance, while cleaning, a friend you haven't heard from in years suddenly contacts you with excellent news.

Predicting the future-TRACE FORWARD

Predicting the future through subtle signs is an advanced technique known as "Trace Forward." This method involves sensing the unfolding of life in any given moment to anticipate when a sudden stroke of good fortune will occur in the future. While mastering this technique typically requires several years of life response, knowledge and experience, it's something anyone can develop over time.

Here is a scenario-

Perfect Timing: Ray's Intuition at Work

One day Ray rather than take his afternoon walk, decided to wait at his office for a FedEx courier package to arrive with his new HP laser printer. For several days, he tracked the package and therefore knew that it would arrive soon. Instead of waiting around for a FedEx package, Ray decided to vacuum the office floor at 2 pm. While cleaning, Ray realised the vacuum cleaner wasn't working properly due to a mistake made during assembly. After fixing it, Ray vacuumed for 15 minutes but was concerned that he would miss the delivery of the printer because of the loud sound of vacuum. Then it occured to Ray that the delivery would arrive as soon as the vacuuming was done. True to his intuition, as soon as the vacuuming was done, the delivery arrived!

This ability to predict the precise moment of a life response is a testament to one's understanding of the flow of events and their experience with life responses. However, it's important for one to approach this method with humility and not let the effort stroke one's ego. Using it for personal gain can invite trouble, but when wielded with humility, it becomes a fascinating and rewarding experience, and further proof that one can move the life and determine the future of life from within!

Equilibrium and Balancing: Developing Subtle Perceptions and navigating in Daily Actions

Throughout the day, we find ourselves engaging in hundreds and thousands of acts in the course of the day, ranging from split-second actions to ones demanding hours of effort. Yet, we tend to move out of balance with it and its needs. This disconnect happens because of our inability to give the act the proper level of attention; the impulses driven by our lower emotional nature, and the tendency to move out of alignment with the Present influenced by the push and pull of past experiences and future expectations.

By developing a subtle awareness and observing attentively, we can discern the precise duration, attention, patience, and precision required for each task to yield a positive outcome. For instance, when washing dishes, we can sense if we're dedicating adequate attention or rushing it in the name of some future action we wish to get to, etc.

Taking a moment to step back, and gauging the level of attention, duration, patience, focus required, one can re engage the act and move forward with the right rhythm, leading to near-perfect results. Furthermore, subsequent actions tend to unfold harmoniously. Through such seemingly mundane activities, we can thus discover the rhythms of the universe and rhythms of life by moving ourselves into perfect alignment with it attracting series of positive life responses.

88

Self-initiatives vs. Life-initiatives

What comes on its own in our life transcends even the Universe. It is from the Supreme. As it is from the Supreme, it sustains.

As we see there is significant power in accepting the conditions life has put before us. This is true for both work situations and other areas of life. When we maintain a positive attitude towards what life offer– whether good or bad on the surface – life will cooperate with us and produce remarkable outcomes.

Life coming to us succeeds -Success is far more likely to occur when we take up an opportunity that comes our way, as opposed to when we initiate our own action.

The most important event in Ray's training career occurred when Ray accepted life's initiative rather than going after his own initiative.

Ray's successful training career

Ray was working at a desktop publishing centre headquarters, where he was the head of dozens of franchisee operations worldwide. One day, his boss asked him to engage in some training for a franchisee at the headquarters. He thought it a pretty trivial use of his time, yet he did it nonetheless. A week or so later, two well-dressed women entered the headquarters location and asked Ray if they could talk in private. They then asked him if he was interested in doing software training classes for their training company. He agreed, and did several classes for the firm, which launched his

25-year most enjoyable training career. Ray realised later that his subconscious aspiration and passion to become a trainer had come to fruition through life's initiative. The boss asking Ray to do training and women coming in were the initiatives of Life, which he acceded to, opening the door to overwhelming career change and significant success.

This illustrates the principle that when Life presents you with work or opportunity, it tends to succeed. Success, in this context, means ease of unfolding, length of time, higher levels of achievement in life, etc.

Life's initiative is a higher calling

Taking up an opportunity usually ends in success, whereas self-initiated endeavours succeed less frequently. The lesson is that if a genuine opportunity arises, you should seriously consider it rather than dismiss or ignore it. It is very often Life summoning you to your higher calling, may be calling of your soul. When we take up that Calling, the result is overwhelmingly likely to succeed.

Few examples of Life-initiatives that Succeed

Here are several ways in which Life-initiatives comes along the way:

Opportunities arise unexpectedly when:

- People appear unexpectedly with an opportunity
- Unsolicited offers for opportunities come your way
- People invite you to participate in projects they've initiated
- Unexpected developments occur where your involvement is needed
- People make important suggestions and recommendations for you to pursue a specific path
- When one is desperate, something emerges in response to a prayer or profound aspiration
- While you are working on something for someone and they ask you to do something else or something more

Few Examples of Our Own Initiatives that Fail

Self-initiated endeavors tend to succeed less often. In other words, when we undertake something on our own, with no obvious sanction of Life, the work tends to succeed less frequently, or with trouble, or may fail altogether after a brief effort.

Failure of man's business due to absence of life-initiatives-Incongruence signals

E.g. One man seeking to increase his income decided to launch a new business. No one had approached him to propose the idea of starting the business or no signal of life's initiative or support in his atmosphere. Though he had a lot of energy and enthusiasm and tried to take the support of others, ultimately the initiative did not succeed. One reason was the lack of a positive atmosphere in the surrounding environment, which was not conducive to the success of this undertaking.

Positive tendencies of Life coming to us indicates real solid chance of success.

Here are some of the certain negative tendencies in ourselves relating to our own Self-initiatives that indicates limited success or even outright failure.

Incongruence signals

- An urge to initiate something without apparent support from others.
- Attempting to revive an old work that had limited success before.
- Broadcasting confidently to others the great opportunity which one sees for success.
- Experiencing eagerness or expectation in our nerves.
- There will be sense of strain, restrain or even push back in such an undertaking.

- There will be an urge and impulsiveness to execute things as we decide and actually do it. When the inner and outer atmosphere is not ripe or conducive and there is a vacuum, to fill the void, it arises from within as an urge or impulse in us. This indicates incongruency.

- Engaging in a task out of desperation rather than genuine commitment and value.

- A positive tending Life-initiative is presenting itself, but you avoid it for your self-chosen initiative by rejecting life-chosen initiative.

Each instance of failed self-initiative provides insights into qualities that hint at longer-term limited success or failure. It's important to note, however, that this doesn't imply all self-initiatives fail; rather, they succeed less frequently compared to Life's initiatives.

Life- initiatives carry the sanction of Life and may even harbor our purpose and destiny within them, radiating an exceptionally positive vibration that often leads to great success. To frame a hypothesis, we can say, self-initiative succeeds at a rate of 50% or less, whereas Life's initiative, when pursued, succeeds at a rate of 75-90%.

<u>Power of Restraint</u>–There is also great power in holding back self-initiative and wait for the life-initiative and watch for the signals from life and the atmosphere whether the events unfolding, resources availability, people's expressions are supporting our self-initiatives or going against it. Identifying such signals by holding back our self-initiative and experimenting will greatly help one in taking decisions and actions. When we hold back thus, Life can respond with marvelous life response oriented results. This life character is called the "Power of Restraint."

Due to past disappointments with a client, Ray restrained himself and did not share the new design which he created to this client. Ray recalled the life principle that self-initiating tends not to work out (whereas Life initiating works out better). Surprisingly, the next day, the same client responded enthusiastically to a post about this new design of Ray in a discussion forum, something he had never done over the course of half a decade, even though Ray had made hundreds of such posts before! This experience underscores the power of Life's initiatives over self-initiated endeavors.

Life's welcome signal or unwelcome signal

Here is one more example of how to watch for life's welcome signal or unwelcome signal. Many times we push, assert, force or insist many things or persons in life. It is wise to watch for life's signals before we resort to such actions.

Life's welcome signal refers to situations where we receive an invitation or indication to proceed, while an unwelcome signal denotes the absence of such an invitation. For instance, in forming new friendships, one typically waits for an invitation to visit someone's home rather than going there without prior invitation. If one ignores this courtesy and shows up uninvited, it can lead to discomfort and misunderstandings. When one expects an invitation and it does not come, one must stop and think why it is so. The person may be hesitant to invite due to several reasons- house not clean, or someone ill in the house or may even think that one is too big a person to visit their house, etc. When the invitation does not come, there is a valid reason and one must respect that reason and refrain from visiting home uninvited. When one violates this, then everything that follows goes wrong.

What is demonstrated by life in miniature with respect to visiting another person's house gets played out in all other areas of life also. Where we see this invitation from life and respond, there we succeed and where we don't see this invitation and still we insist on taking initiatives, there we fail. Resist to Insist is wise.

Failure of man's painting business

A man relocated across the country with aspirations to launch a house painting business, driven by his own initiative, only to encounter failure. Later, a family friend offered him a position at one of their chain stores, leading to a remarkable series of positive and successful outcomes that transformed his life. That is the power of responding to Life's initiatives rather than taking one's own. It is a power of stillness and silence in which we wait for life to take us to the next level.

Life's Initiatives and the Aspiration of Our Soul

From a spiritual perspective, the truth is what our soul aspires for evolution in this birth comes as the calling of Life to us. As life's initiative is aligned with our soul's aspiration, when we embrace what life places before us, events unfold harmoniously bringing us great joy and success. Self-initiatives emerge from our lower faculties—mind, heart, and body—yielding results that are often limited in scope and impact. One can examine their own life past and current events from this perspective and experiment further to gain more insight into this subtle life-truth. Furthermore, if we can develop this knowledge, we can consciously apply it in work and the rest of our lives, to accelerate our evolution, and that of the interest and intent of our Evolving Being, Soul.

Acceptance of Life Initiative Spreads and Connects to others

What Comes To You Spreads & Astonishes. Whatever comes to you through life initiative is of universal dimension and carries the intention of not only your progress but the progress of others too. As life initiative is comprehensive, when you accept what life sends you and cooperate by embracing the life initiative and act forward, such acts will invariably be successful, and will also surprisingly connect with others' interests thereafter. They will say that it is an astonishing coincidence that you brought up that matter just at that particular time when they were experiencing the same or they found it helpful. The deeper truth is that you have tapped into a vibrant wave of knowledge or information, becoming its recent caretaker, benefitting from it, and then passing it on to others. This is the Universal Force in action which acts through Life. Our initiatives emerge from tunnel vision, while Life's initiatives come from peripheral vision. One is myopic; the latter is telescopic.

89

Perceiving and embracing opportunities behind Negative

By separating ourselves from life, we lose the totality of our vision of Reality and see things in bits and pieces. Reality includes all positive and negative and we have the opportunity to learn from all that life has put before us. Having the vision of Reality will make us see the utility of the positive and negative in the process of moving life forward. By this way, we can broaden our being in every dimension. By embracing and remaining positively open towards the ALL, increases our receptivity to the Spirit's Force and attracts greater life responses. All life can be viewed as a field of opportunity and adventure. Every negative is a disguised positive. Every point of negative is a means of the positive.

We should remain vigilant to recognise and embrace the opportunities which come our way. Those who embrace opportunity tend to accomplish more than those who do not recognise and embrace the opportunity. They will be on the fast-track of success. There are unique moments in one's life that pass like a cloud. One must catch them on the wing, for they never return. Opportunities sail silently and they don't come by announcing. Even recognition of opportunities requires a great level of heightened perception. Many people remain ignorant of the opportunities which have come in their life and gone. Many people recognise the loss of opportunity after it has gone. Few people remain blissfully unaware and ignorant of the opportunity which has come and also gone in their life. The opportunities would have gone like the clouds above the head. It is totally out of their mental radar. It is total unconsciousness. Life coming to us with an opportunity should never be ignored. In such cases of positive response by us to life by accepting the incoming opportunity, life tends to bring more opportunities and good fortune in one's life. For this one has to perceive all life events positively.

Many times people don't take up an opportunity because something in their attitude blocks it. They may perceive some negatives associated with the opportunity and tend to avoid it. However if one can manage to overcome the wanting attitude, and embrace the opportunity in full, life rewards one and even the perceived negatives associated with the situation quickly disappear.

Embracing Change in Training Leads to Unexpected Success

Fully cooperating with the unexpected life situations can evoke startling positive conditions. This is one type of life response which happens when we embrace the opportunity behind the seemingly negative situation.

Once Ray, as trainer, encountered an unexpected turn of events in a training session. Things were moving along quite smoothly. Unexpectedly during the end of the session, a higher-up suddenly came into the classroom and suggested altering the direction of the instruction. Initially though Ray was taken aback by the abrupt change, he decided to embrace it. Despite Ray's earlier fears and misgivings, suddenly everything started moving to a higher level. There was increased energy, enthusiasm, and involvement among the participants. By the end of the session, everyone was practically dancing on air! This experience taught Ray that by letting go of fears of the unknown and wholeheartedly embracing and cooperating with changes in the flow of events, life responded positively, as if all were carried on a wave of great success! Ray's perception of the higher-up's intervention as a positive sign instead of negative sign turned the direction in which things unfolded. By accepting the alteration in the direction of the instructions, Ray gained the capability to alter the direction of the session outcomes in a more intense positive way.

Two Inner Approaches that Will take you to a Whole New Level of Success

It is always learning to see things in a positive aspect which come to us negatively.

The Problem

Many people struggle to reach their full potential because they fail to recognise how their inner world affects their outer reality. They fail to understand how their inner condition directly blocks further accomplishment in life.

There are at least two major approaches to resolving this problem.

Approach 1: Transforming Negative Situations

One is to look at negative circumstances occurring outside one's self, and make the necessary corresponding inner adjustment.

- Identify negative events in your life.
- Reflect on your own thoughts and behaviours related to those situations.
- Make a conscious effort to change negativity into a positive attitude or action.

According to the principle of "inner-outer correspondence," this shift will attract positive experiences from the world around you.

Approach 2: Self-Inventory and Improvement

- Evaluate your own strengths and weaknesses.
- Identify areas where you can improve, such as organisation, skills, work ethic, or life balance.
- Develop a plan to address these shortcomings and make a dedicated effort to implement it.
- As you transform your inner self, your outer world will respond with positive changes, mirroring your inner growth.

Let's say you decide to do a personal inventory. You examine various aspects of your life, like how organised you are, your skill set, your work ethic, and your overall outlook. You also consider your inner strength, if your current job aligns with your desires, and if you're embracing life's challenges. Through this self-evaluation, you discover areas for improvement. Maybe your living space and work area are cluttered, your goals lack focus, you tend to procrastinate, and you struggle with punctuality. The next step is to create a plan to address these shortcomings. With dedication and commitment, you put the plan into action. As you work on becoming a more organised, focused, and punctual person, you'll start to see positive changes in your external world. This reflects the concept of "Life Response" – your outer world mirroring the improvements you're making within yourself.

Harnessing Positivity: How Attitudes and Actions Shape Our Lives

- Expressing negative attitudes attracts negative circumstances.

- Staying fully positive or raising your level of cheerfulness and enthusiasm attracts positive conditions.

- Focusing your thoughts, interests, and emotions on something tends to bring more of it into your life.

- Deeply aspiring to achieve something prompts life to conspire to make it happen quickly.

- Committing to a course of action, i.e., making a decision causes life to move in your favour.

- Life also responds positively to taking physical action.

90

Correlating Negative to Ourselves

- Pinpointing the ignorance in others causes our own ignorance to grow.
- Observing the knowledge in others causes our own knowledge to grow.

How to relate to the negative circumstances that come our way?

From the laws of life response, we already know that negative happenings in our external world often reflect some negative quality inside ourselves. Furthermore, if we identify and transform this internal negativity, the external circumstances will swiftly respond positively in return.

We often attract negative circumstances in our lives due to the fact that we ourselves are acting negatively in another area of our lives. Recognising the connection of one area to a seemingly unrelated other area indicates an expanding consciousness. Understanding how to address this and witnessing the positive results makes us wiser, building more faith in the Inner-Outer Correspondence and gives greater knowledge in Correlating Negative to Ourselves and emerging into zones of Higher Positivity.

Beyond Conflict and Contradictions: The Hidden Power of Opposites

While positive thinking attracts positive experiences, there's another layer to consider. The contradiction between opposing ideas, people, or entities (organisations, nations, etc.) can also spark growth. When we examine conflicts more closely, we realise that the contradiction holds the potential for new progress.

For example, when one conflicts with another person over certain ideas, often one discovers new, important concepts beyond their beliefs and petty differences. Through these conflicts, one learns about their own limitations, such as a lacking habit, attitude, opinion, or belief. This suggests that what we perceive as conflict and contradiction is actually a complementary, helpful relationship in disguise. The opposing party, though initially perceived as an antagonist, can be a hidden friend in your journey of self-discovery. This startling principle of existence is termed as "Contradictions are Truly Complements." Thus, what we perceive as contradiction, division, and conflict with others through our surface view of things is actually an emerging Higher Harmony from a deeper viewpoint.

Turning Misunderstandings into Insights

A man struggled to get the right information from another person, repeatedly trying without success and going in circles. To break the deadlock, the first man created a list of examples for the other person to follow. This process resulted in sample data that the first man could now share with various other users, which was a welcome development. Additionally, this effort prompted the second person to voluntarily forward a paper revealing much information about himself; something the first man did not ask for, but helped him understand the second man's mind. Ultimately, the misunderstanding had the net effect of creating a better grasp of the process and data required, as well as greater knowledge of the second person.

Life often evolves through seemingly conflictive situations. Life always has a higher purpose in view and secretly aims to bring about greater understanding all around from an evolutionary point of view. If we can recognise the hidden higher harmony in any negative, conflictive, or divisive situation, we can avoid much difficulty and strife. By seeing complementarity instead of contradiction, we can adopt the right mindset and develop effective strategies, moving life rapidly forward: to a higher level of success, well-being, happiness and joy.

The Positive Value of Negative People

Positive people add positive value to our lives, but what about negative individuals? According to the laws of life, we only encounter what we invite into our lives. The invitation is subtle. A negative person around me in the office or at home is there because something deep in me has a spiritual need for their presence. By avoiding a negative person, we are avoiding our inner ignorance to change as inner knowledge.

Avoidance represents austerity, while acceptance is prosperity. To accept and transcend is the way to outgrow. A negative person reveals aspects of ourselves, that we may be unaware of or unwilling to accept. He tells us by his jealousy that there is jealousy in us. This is the positive value of a negative person.

Facing Our Shadows: How Negative People Can Help Us Grow

Avoiding a negative person keeps our inner ignorance at bay, preventing it from transforming into knowledge. As long as we avoid the person representing that ignorance, we miss the opportunity for progress. That negative individual is there for us to make progress. When we make that progress, mysteriously the individual vanishes from our life or the botheration created by the individual stops. Often, we are not aware of this or unwilling to acknowledge it. The moment we recognise this and show a willingness to abandon the inner negative trait, life brings a positive response.

Transforming Resentment into Opportunity-The Christmas Party Paradox

Years ago, Ray's friend during her company's annual Christmas party, attended with high hopes of winning a prize, as she had in previous years. However, when another woman won the grand prize, Ray's friend felt a pang of disappointment. It wasn't just the loss of the prize that troubled her; it was also the fact that the winner was someone she had clashed with previously.

Upon returning home, she received news of her family members facing unexpected difficulties. Sensing a connection between her reaction at the party and this negative event, Ray gently broached the topic with her the next day. Ray then suggested that if she overcame her ill-will towards the woman, good things would start happening. Fortunately, Ray's friend was familiar with this inner approach – having seen it produce powerful results in the past – and therefore agreed to take up Ray's challenge and agreed to let go of her resentment towards the other woman.

To Ray's surprise, on Christmas morning, Ray's friend presented him with an expensive iPod, explaining that it was a gift from her employer. Curious about the sudden turn of events, Ray delved deeper into the situation. Ray's friend revealed that she had taken the initiative to congratulate the woman who won the prize, despite their past conflict. It was clear to Ray that the free IPod gift she received from the company was a direct response to her own initiative to make amends with the other woman.

As they discussed further, Ray's friend disclosed that the iPods were actually gifts for all employees. It became evident that her act of goodwill had far-reaching effects beyond just herself. Her reversal of attitude by overcoming her negative feelings and extending kindness, attracted a mass life response result for the entire collective of individuals she was part of!

Learning from Positive Experiences

Just like negative experiences, we can learn from positive ones too.

- Identify a moment of sudden good fortune in your life.

- Reflect on your own recent actions or behaviours, both internal (thoughts, attitudes) and external (actions).

- Look for a connection between your positive behaviour and the fortunate outcome.

- Once you identify this link, try to replicate the positive behaviour consistently.

For instance, if you experience a positive outcome that frees you from a tough situation, reflect on how your selfless actions towards a friend contributed to it. Armed with this understanding, continue to prioritise selflessness, thereby perpetuating the occurrence of miracles in your life!

Removing the Mental, Vital Barriers

Selfishness, competitiveness, laziness, jealousy, vanity, the pursuit of prestige, stubborn insistence, meanness, stinginess, fear, doubts, disbelief, unconsciousness, and various other mental and vital barriers hinder accomplishment. To achieve success, it's essential to eliminate these barriers. Those aspiring for prosperity should overcome selfishness and jealousy to take joy in the prosperity and the happiness of others. Similarly, those who want to achieve results should relinquish vanity, self-importance, and the quest for prestige. To conquer external barriers like fierce competition, a declining market or the negativity of other people, one should shift their faith from outside to inside and remove the inner barriers.

Make a list of several negative things in your life. Find the corresponding wrong attitudes, habits, beliefs, or behaviours that led to these negatives. Once identified, work to reverse these factors, as doing so will often lead to the swift disappearance of the external negatives.

91

Personality and Receptivity

A person's personality is a complex of mental, nervous and physical habits held together by a number of dominant ideas, desires and associations. Every action, how simple or how small, carries the stamp of a person's consciousness. The whole personality is revealed even in the smallest work to those who have the knowledge to perceive it.

Energy, ability, opinion, attitude or character alone or in combination do not determine the results of action. It is consciousness and personality. As is the consciousness and personality, so is the result. As we rise in consciousness, we rise in personality.

Raising one's Personality

How to raise one's personality?

Skills, abilities, talents, diligence, intelligence, memory are partial abilities that can only contribute to the achievement of personality and do not directly raise one's personality. Then what can raise? It is Values. Yes, VALUES raise one's personality and strengthens it. Values (Non reaction, psychological equilibrium, seeing other person's perspective, attention, increasing energy level, integrity, aspiration for growth, gratitude, taking responsibility, time conscious etc..) which are spiritual skills can raise the personality. Universe and Life comes to us as Values. Embracing higher values, directly raises our consciousness and personality and brings us greater LIFE RESPONSE and GOOD FORTUNE in life.

Receptivity raises the Personality

Human endowments are in layers. These endowments are Values, Character, Skills, Capabilities, Behaviours, Manners. Human personality is the product of physiological and psychological conditioning. The fabric of human personality can be reconstituted by increasing the receptivity to higher consciousness and power. As in the endowment layer, Values are higher and deeper, by embracing Values, one can easily reconstitute and reshape the lower layers below Values namely Character, Skills, Capabilities, Behaviours, Manners. Whenever higher acts on lower, it influences all the lower layers of being and hence great results come in a short time. Time is abridged by this direct transformation. To transform is to shift from one extreme of one's nature to the other, lower nature to higher nature. Values increase our receptivity which in turn raises our personality.

Everyone has receptivity within. It is buried deep. Receptivity within oneself is endless. Only one has to open oneself from within and allow for the wisdom to flower in their being. OPEN-ALLOW- BLOSSOM. This is the direct way to raise the Personality and its endowments of Values, Character, Skills, Capabilities, Behaviours, Manners. Personality is the main driver.

Personality is the determinant of Accomplishment

There is no limit to what life can give us, only our current limited capacity to receive. As we intensify our receptivity to the Spiritual force inside us, we find that inner disharmonies diminish and thus outer disharmonies disappear by themselves. Ultimately it is the Personality which determines the accomplishment, not talents or capacities or even values.

Personality is the central element of a person which is open and receptive to new experiences. Character reacts, while personality is an unstructured human energy that thrives on life's challenges, curiosity, and the urge to act. Manners are what is exhibited for others. Manners can develop into behaviour through values. Behaviour is what one believes they should exhibit. Behaviour is changeable and unorganised. Behaviour can be developed into character through commitment. Character is structured. A person can change his behaviour, not his character. Character means that the emotions have accepted an idea from the mind. Characters won't change after that. Personality transcends character. Most people lack true behaviour, and without personality, one's accomplishments will be limited to what their father achieved. Personality encompasses the whole being, whereas talents and capacities are partial. Every accomplished person has a developed personality, enabling success across any field, unlike specific skills or talents which are limited to particular fields. In life, each moment presents various options, and the way one responds shapes their future.

How we react will determine our future. That which makes the choice is the personality in life and nature. In the soul, the psychic makes the choice. The psychic is the soul in nature. Choices shape both personality and our future.

Rapid Personality Growth: From Unconsciousness to Consciousness through SPIRIT

Any process that takes centuries in life can occur in a split second in Spirit. What you choose spiritually and consciously enables rapid growth. If you are spiritually unconscious, you must recognise the level of your unconsciousness. **How to become conscious when you are unconscious?**

1. Identify your current state.

2. Shift towards the positive aspect of that state.

3. Develop perfect skill and transform it into a talent.

4. Do not become attached to your talents. Aspire to reach the next higher level, and exhaust your energies at this level to go to the next higher level.

Receptivity of Soul-A Woman Healed by Faith in Spirit

Once a woman developed an intense, acute pain for which medicine offered no relief. The pain became unbearable. She knew nothing about the Spirit's force and when she began to hear about the method of invocation of the Spirit, she developed faith in the Spirit's power. She was surprised to find that none of her prayers to the Spirit went unanswered. One day, someone gave her husband a flower, and for about ten days, he brought it home. A friend explained to her about the significance of the flowers, mentioning the Prosperity flower. She vaguely remembered that the flower her husband had been bringing was called Nagalingam, also known as 'Prosperity'. During those ten days, her modest beauty parlour started earning Rs. 1000 per day.

Her faith in the Spirit grew, and she decided to pray to Spirit to relieve her neck pain, despite doctors' negative opinions. One day, she sat in meditation and felt a powerful force entering her left hand, which frightened her, causing her to stop. Despite the fear, she yearned for the experience again, recognising it as the Force entering her body. She resumed meditation, and the Force alternately frightened and fascinated her. Remarkably, her neck pain vanished completely and never returned.

This miraculous event marked a significant moment in her life. The Force that enters can frighten people, as it is very strong. But the fascination it brings often overcomes the fear. The human part of us may be scared, but the soul is receptive and enjoys the touch of the Spirit's Divine Force.

The Astrologer and Server

An astrologer entertained himself at a hotel table by making predictions. Turning to the server, he remarked, "Your hand is lucky." However, the humble server possessed a wisdom surpassing the astrologer's expectations. He replied, "Sir, what does luck mean to a man like me? Maybe I would get four idlis instead of the present two idlis."

Personality determines the receptivity of LUCK

Usually, we anticipate that talents will be rewarded. We admire skills, honor capacity, and cherish talents. However, when the time for reward arrives, it is not necessarily proportional to our abilities or talents, but rather according to our status and Personality. Intelligence, memory, hard work, skill, capacity, knowledge, and the like, no matter how impressive, are only partial endowments. These partial capacities can contribute but not accomplish by themselves. **Responsibility, seriousness, patience, strength of character, and the incapacity to react—i.e., equanimity—** comprise Personality. Generally, Personality goes with status, high birth or something outstanding in one. Even if luck favours someone, it often manifests differently depending on their Personality. For instance, luck might translate into receiving four idlis for a hotel server, while for the son of a mill owner, it could mean obtaining a Ministerial position. **God bestows GRACE as LUCK, but Personality prunes LUCK to its own size.**

Organise The Personality To Suit The Incoming Opportunities

Our development is an expression of our capacity to inwardly organise ourselves. For higher accomplishment we have to raise our skill of organisation. Individual progresses by becoming conscious of greater opportunities, releasing their energy to avail of the opportunities and organising these energies for maximum efficiency and accomplishment. In effect, it involves organising one's personality.

Organising one's personality involves directing thoughts, energy, and actions towards higher achievements, removing barriers in understanding and attitude that divert the energy or hinder action, fully utilising all capacities and resources to accomplish the goal, ensuring that all attitudes and behaviours are consistent (coordinated) with the goal, and eliminating all ways in which one's energy is wasted and dissipated.

Expression of Personality through our terminal of Temperament

The utmost significance of human existence is the **temperamental end of expression**. Temperament is the terminal end through which our personality expresses itself. Any changes in character or personality become evident through shifts in temperament.

Transforming Temperament: A Collaborative Effort

The four elements in the transformation are

1. The Witnessing Soul
2. Personality
3. Character
4. Mastery Over Character

To bring about the slightest change in the temperament, one needs proportionate mastery over the character, consent in the personality and sanction of the soul. The witnessing soul must sanction for the change, the personality must consent, the ingrained traits of character must agree to dissolve and re-constitute the grain. This in turn requires a mastery to reshape our character, ultimately influencing temperament.

Receptivity and Capacity of Retention

In Tamil, a character in a story is referred to as a vessel that fully receives the inspiration of the author within their own context. Receptivity equates to retentiveness; to receive and retain requires willingness and a capacity to retain. Those who comprehend contents of the book "The Life Divine" often expresses the challenge of retaining the contents in the mind of what is received in the mind while reading. Receptive mind mass is necessary to retain new information, similar to the difficulty, learners face while learning foreign languages. Despite fully receiving Spirit's grace, retaining it proves challenging due to the innate resistance of nature to accept and retain anything new. However, Spirit's grace persists within us through the inner endorsement of our personality and nature.

Spirit builds Character and Personality

Man's character is the psychological organisation through which he functions. His values and spiritual skills shape his character. Men of strong character are men of accomplishment. Character offers high accomplishment.

Invocation of the Spirit may bring immediate luck, but it gradually contributes to the development of character and personality in anyone. The Spirit enables one to recognise the presence of luck and demonstrates that it is attainable. However, what comes in serves to fulfill the work on hand and cannot stay. For luck to stay forever, there must be a fabric of personality that can retain it. This foundation is character, which is an organisation of inner energies into that fabric.

92

Equilibrium of Energies

Energy possesses strength, a vibratory frequency, and a direction. For every action, there is an equal and opposite reaction. Each energy sent forth, attracts an energy of equal intensity and vibratory quality. Every force seeks to perpetuate and multiply itself.

Energies in Nature

All energies in Nature must have their natural consequence. As is the nature of the energies so must be the nature of the results. Contact of force with force generates action and reaction. We call this the Law of Karma having good and evil consequences. But good and evil are relative terms. All action, knowingly or unknowingly moves toward an ultimate Good beyond all relativities. Nature permits wide swings, but ultimately restores a balance.

Equilibrium of energies attracts positive life response

If nothing is irresistible to us and if we can maintain equilibrium of our energies, life will lose its capacity to bring negative responses in our life. Equilibrium in our inner can attract only positive life responses. If one can control one's sensations, it can bring infinite power within oneself. It demands a great discipline. Discipline is the mental organisation of the capacity. Discipline is the capacity to control impulses.

Equilibrium aids Accomplishment

A work is accomplished through the harmony of its components and the equilibrium of the energies within the field. The human body is the best example of this principle. How is health maintained, and why does disease arise? **Equilibrium is health. Disease is because of disharmony.** The body exists in successive stages of physical, vital, mental and spiritual energies. These rules apply to each plane; however, when the Centre of a person rises from the physical to the vital, the deficiencies of the physical are largely offset by vital energies. Yet, there is a limit.

Hunger of the body can be held at bay for hours if the vitality of the company is attractive. But a LIMIT is there. As we raise our equilibrium at each level of our existence (physical, vital, mental and spiritual) we attract corresponding positive energies of higher planes and further the energies of higher planes energises the lower planes and the outer atmosphere aiding for rapid manifestation of our potentials and accomplishment. Invocation of Spirit empowers one with spiritual energies for lightning-like accomplishment by attracting the infinite in one's life.

Redirecting, Reversal, Consecration of ENERGIES towards INNER

Energies continuously arise and flow outward in a life movement of expansion and expression known as manifestation. The greater the energy, the greater the individual. For one who aspire for conscious rapid evolution and transformation, one must capture these energies as they manifest in the form of thoughts, feelings, impulses, etc., and, through an act of will and concentration, reverse their direction inward. **Reversed thoughts lead to Silence; reversed feelings lead to detachment; reversed impulses lead to power.** Just as breathing is an essential, continuous function for life, this constant concentration is essential for conscious evolution and transformation. The foundation for this relies on accumulated energy being redirected to the Centre.

Spiritual Energies for ABUNDANCE and PROSPERITY

The above referred energy which is generated by redirection and reversal of thoughts, feelings, impulses is neutral, not inherently spiritual, and becomes spiritual only when offered to the inner Divine and its service. When such inward oriented energies are **consecrated to the Spirit**, the powers of the Spirit burst forth within oneself and place one in an atmosphere of ABUNDANCE and PROSPERITY.

Managing Energy and Ego: Holding within New Stores of Energies

New stores of energy, if left unharnessed and unchecked, can quickly lead to movements of the Ego. This is evident in various situations. For instance, someone who has been sick feels much better and then wastes their newfound energy in unnecessary conversations, where they needlessly recollect and narrate unimportant, even trivial moments of their past, with a certain type of self-congratulation. The Ego takes over with this surge of energy, and as a result the energy normally gets depleted in the process.

We often see this in young people, when they feel a surge of energy, but then waste it engaging in questionable activities that satisfy the lower Ego. They usually lack self-awareness of their energy status, let alone control it. If they were more self-aware, this energy could sustain and build up further, attracting enormous opportunities. Thus remembering to stay balanced and humble will also keep new stores of energy flowing and expanding.

The challenge is that we are usually too unconscious to recognise these aspects of our being—whether related to energy, Ego, or humility. If you have a genuine insight or idea, refrain from broadcasting it. Hold it deep inside—silently, quietly, and without expectation. This internal holding builds up energy and power, increasing the likelihood of its realisation in due time.

93

Energy and Accomplishment

Levels of Accomplishment

There are four fundamental levels at which an individual can accomplish – survival, growth, development, and evolution or transformation.

1. *Survival*: Living at the survival level one has a conscious or unconscious desire to remain at the present level of achievement in life. There is no attempt to rise above one's present achievement, nor is there an effort to raise one's own personal abilities. There is neither a quantitative expansion nor a qualitative movement to a potential higher level.

   A real world example of accomplishment at the level of survival is an instructor who has achieved a level of success that keeps them comfortable, has a certain skill set, and has no desire or effort to get more work or perhaps even upgrade their skills to meet the current needs of their students.

2. *Growth*: Growth, on the other hand, refers to enhancing one's current level of achievement. This can be seen in actions like improving a skill, gaining more knowledge in the same or a different field at the same level, and increasing earnings through greater effort. Essentially, you are achieving more, but within the same scope. It represents a **horizontal expansion** at the same level of capability and accomplishment. For an instructor to grow, they would update their knowledge by learning the latest versions of the programs they currently teach and seek out work with other companies to teach the

same things he has been teaching in the past. He would be aspiring for more of the same work.

3. ***Development***: Development signifies advancing to a higher level of achievement. This can involve acquiring new or advanced skills, embracing and applying higher personal values, transforming negative attitudes into positive ones, gaining deeper knowledge, developing new beliefs, or generally responding from a higher centre than one's current level of development and consciousness. These actions represent personal development, where you achieve at a higher level rather than just more at the same level. Therefore, it is considered a **vertical expansion** to a new level of capacity and accomplishment.

In a practical example, at the level of development, an instructor might aspire to teach entirely new subjects beyond their usual curriculum, connect with different types of clients to offer these new courses, write a book on the new subject area, adjust personal attitudes (such as those towards superiors), or more fully integrate a cherished value into their work, such as ensuring students gain real knowledge rather than just enjoying the experience.

4. ***Evolution***: Evolution represents an ascent to a significantly higher level of consciousness and state of being. For instance, an emotionally driven person might transition from being dominated by desires and attachments to embodying more refined or elevated emotions. Alternatively, they could evolve from being primarily emotional to becoming more intellectual and contemplative, shifting their life focus from emotional intensity to thoughtfulness. This evolution might also involve acquiring spiritual capacities, such as the ability to experience knowledge as illuminations of light or intuition, or to find his personal evolving soul, the psychic being.

In these instances, you are achieving from a higher plane of consciousness than before. It represents a vertical leap to a new level of capacity and accomplishment; an elevation of one's being to a whole new higher plane of consciousness.

For example, at the level of evolution, an instructor could change from being a person who competently performs his courses in an orderly and efficient manner to an individual who is passionate about teaching and emotionally identified with his students. They could develop entirely new instructional theories based on his new level of consciousness, rather than merely being a teacher of existing ideas. Their overall attitude toward work would shift positively, moving from emotional interactions with students to a deeper understanding, possibly incorporating spiritual methods as a foundation for his work.

Transformation

At the frontiers of the development of the being is the transformation of the individual to an entirely different mode of functioning in life. This can involve embodying a permanent inner change that connects one to their inner, soul being; enabling a spiritual transformation to higher spiritual planes beyond the mind; or achieving the ultimate Supramental transformation into a completely new type of being, surpassing current human capabilities. As we embody these three transformational frontiers, we open to the infinite potentials of life, where we can thus accomplish infinitely in life.

Pause and Reflect

1. Assess Your Current Level:

*Identify if you are at survival, growth, development, evolution, or transformation.

*Most people are at the survival level.

2. Plan Your Progression:

Survival to Growth: Improve existing skills or expand knowledge.

Growth to Development: Acquire new skills or adopt higher values.

***Development to Evolution:** Elevate consciousness and develop new methods.

***Evolution to Transformation:** Embrace permanent inner changes and spiritual growth.

3. *Observe Others:*

*Identify people who have moved from growth to development or made evolutionary leaps.

*Study their history and strategies.

*Consider how you can apply similar changes in your life.

CONSCIOUS ENERGY

To know the results is not knowledge. One must know the energy that created those results. Energy, once released, fulfills its purpose. Energy decides. Energy alone decides. Energy comes from WILL. Self-conception releases energy. Scientists question whether this energy is conscious. Their efforts focus on enhancing its efficiency to perform more work. Energy that grows in efficiency is considered conscious energy. Consciousness itself is creative, generating energy. Emotion energises.

CALL THE ENERGY

It is wise not to undertake any important work when physical or psychological energy is below average, since the results of the work depend far more on the energy level than on the correctness of the actions taken. Simple technique for raising one's energy level is to call the energy by invoking your inner spirit. Open yourself psychologically and invoke energy to descend and enter into your personality.

Conversion of energies for accomplishment

Evolution from one plane to another demands conversion of energy on the scale of liquids becoming vapour. Crossing the plane, energy explodes. Like how deeply rooted trees can absorb more water and produce greater yields, when we are deeply rooted in our inner core, we can draw more on the cosmic energies, divine wisdom and accomplish more.

Achieving self-fulfillment is an accomplishment. High energy serves as the fuel and driving force behind great achievements, inspiring and motivating people to put forth their best efforts. Energy is the foundation of all creativity, acting as the fuel that ignites the fire of inspiration. The more fuel we have, the more we can achieve. Children possess an almost limitless supply of energy, but as we age, we often lose much of the enthusiasm and energy of our youth. However, this decline is not inevitable. There are numerous ways to restore our youthful energy or increase our current energy levels, enabling us to achieve great things and find true fulfillment in life.

Energy and Innovation-Edison's Energy and Accomplishment

Energy spurs innovation. No other individual has been as instrumental in generating immense wealth as Thomas Alva Edison. Edison was a tireless worker, often going days without sleep to produce 1,100 patentable inventions and create several entirely new industries, including motion pictures, phonographs and recording, and electric and household appliances. The General Electric Company, which he founded, is one of the largest industrial corporations in the United States. In 1907, at the age of 60, Hearst's Cosmopolitan magazine encouraged him to authorise a serialised autobiography. "***When I go into senile decay I may consider the autobiographical scheme,***" Edison replied, "but as long as I can put in eighteen hours daily, I don't want to waste any time on it."

Exhaustive Expenditure of All One's Energy Attracts More Energy

There is a strong link between effort and energy:

When you put in a full, all-out effort, even to the point of exhaustion, you tap into a wellspring of energy you never knew you had. Additionally, by discarding any self-doubt and fully committing to the task at hand, you access a vast reservoir of energy just beneath the surface.

A Consultant's Story

Few years ago, a consultant traveled to Europe to meet with various computer software companies. The schedule was tight, and on the last day of the tour, there was an important meeting in Paris with a major software company. As the consultant entered their corporate office, he realised he was completely drained, having traveled for two exhausting weeks.

Recognising that this was the most crucial meeting of the trip, the consultant knew he needed energy to make it successful. He began to intensely call upon the Divine Force and Spirit from the heart centre (emotional being), asking for energy. Within ten minutes he felt like somebody had pumped him up from within. He felt buoyant and charged with energy. He met the Vice President of the company for one hour, and this meeting turned out to be the most effective of all meetings he had during his two weeks tour in Europe and the Vice President was very excited by the consultant's business proposal.

Invoking the Spiritual force is a spiritual approach to being energised when one is listless and without energy. We have access to a universal power to energise ourselves when we are devoid of energy. When we invoke our inner spirit, we are energised to no end.

The capacity to accomplish is infinitely multiplied by shifting from the outer to the inner and from there to the inner which includes the outer.

When problems arise, converting them into opportunities requires greater energy and purification. In this way, problems become a means for our progress, making it essential to address them properly.

Energy that comes from action is liveliness. For an accomplishment at a higher level, energy should come from Silence. That energy leads to quiet efficiency.

All accomplishment is by commensurate concentration of energy. Such concentration is accompanied by patience that is equality. Patience understands that eternity is available for achievement. Such patience is infinite patience. Despite this, such patience possesses the organised energy to accomplish tasks immediately. If one can hold infinite patience as well as organised concentrated energy, one can accomplish the tasks at the same moment.

There is a subtle, almost miraculous relationship between our inner selves and the world around us. When we change the inner, the outer instantly responds. By constant inner work, we grow more conscious of ourselves and life around us and know how to conserve and multiply our energies by tapping into our inner. When we are filled with energy, we accomplish more and attract positive responses from life. Increased energy leads to greater results.

Given the powerful results that can be achieved by making these changes, it makes sense to take up the challenge. Identify areas where you are deficient, and make a concerted effort to implement those changes in your life. If you do, life will immediately start working in your favour.

94

Knowledge+Will+Force= Accomplishment

Is knowledge alone sufficient for accomplishment? If not, what forms must knowledge take before it manifests as results? Is Will and Force required to convert knowledge into action?

Will: The determination and intent to use the knowledge effectively.

Force: The energy and effort required to implement the knowledge.

Both will and force are essential for converting knowledge into tangible outcomes. Without the drive (will) and the necessary effort (force), knowledge remains theoretical and does not lead to accomplishment.

There is only one process of accomplishment, one process governing all CREATION–individual, collective and universal. It is the process by which the finite reveals the Infinite. All human achievements are based on certain fundamental principles. If you know the principles, you have the knowledge needed to accomplish anything. **If anything is to be achieved for the world, it is to be accomplished first inside.**

Knowledge Vs. Faith

Faith is the hidden knowledge of the soul. Faith is the reflection of the soul's knowledge on the mind. We have to act on faith till faith becomes knowledge. Effort is physical, knowledge is mental, but faith is of the

Soul; hence superior to both. Man's effort accumulates as knowledge and the essence of knowledge collects as faith.

Faith in the Spirit Accomplishes Vastly

A lady had been suffering from asthma for over a decade. She was extraordinarily polite and fiercely independent, seeking help only from her children. Hospitalisation was an annual occurrence, sometimes lasting for weeks or months, and the physical suffocation was unbearable for her. During one such hospital visit, the doctors deemed her case hopeless and refused to treat her. Her faith in the Divine Force, whom she believed would save her life and alleviate her pain, began to waver. Unable to pray for her life anymore, she shifted her mindset and prayed for an end to her suffering. She called her children, removed the IV tubes, and refused further medication. She made a profound declaration to her children, "I can't live anymore. Divine will protect you both. Have faith in The Divine." Her children broke into tears, but she felt a weight lift off her mind and fell asleep.

When she woke up, she experienced no suffocation. Her face was bright, and her voice was clear. The attending nurse was astonished and reported it to the doctors, who were incredulous and rushed to offer treatment. The lady chose to go home instead. Over the next fifteen years, hospitalisations became rare. This is an example of negative faith—she prayed to die, but the Divine granted her health and life. Positive faith, even when it sees no immediate response, carries the attitude, "I have done my best. The pain is unrelenting. No prayer to Divine will be in vain, even if the results are not visible. My duty is to exhaust my prayer of faith and not despair. The best will happen to me." Such faith yields the same results but in a higher manner, with no recurrence of the issue. A positive Faith brings positive opportunities, while negative faith merely wards off existing problems. Those who connect with the Spirit have a greater chance of developing positive faith. Faith in the Divine Spirit accomplishes vastly.

Worry arises from a lack of faith. Faith can be understood as the knowledge of the Soul. A person whose soul knows he will get a job has faith, reflected in his mind as a sense of calm assurance. With this faith, he remains calm and secures the job effortlessly.

When faith is absent, a person craves intensity and starts to worry. His imagination supplies him all possible developments about his future. They are gloomy. It develops in all avenues of life. This constant feeding of his imagination results in a barrage of frightening images. No amount of consolation can help such a person because his inner life is filled with turmoil. Ultimately, he gets what he subconsciously sought: intensity.

Can such a person be helped? Most individuals will listen to sound advice. Understanding this truth can gradually help their minds break free from the cycle of worry. However, for those who stubbornly cling to their illusions, there is little hope.

Faith is a great power, especially in the physical. So great an attainment as Brahmic consciousness is not capable of generating FAITH in the mind, not to speak of the body. Nirvikalpasamadhi did not give Swami Vivekananda faith in his guru. Indians who have innate Faith in the Spirit have it as a spiritual inheritance. To draw on that faith is great. To create that faith in oneself is greater still. **Faith** brings in Grace; absence of **faith** in one's capacities brings in Super Grace. **Faith** is created by perseverance. Faith is pure. It is not dependent on other things. If the faith is pure and total, the results are phenomenal.

Expectations neutralise the vast powers of faith one has. For faith to become pure and powerful expectations are to be dropped. Perseverance and patience are to be embraced.

Shifting the reliance from method or medium to the SPIRIT accomplishes vastly. Such pure faith requires pure WILL and pure FORCE for vast ACCOMPLISHMENT.

The Process Of Creation And Accomplishment

All creation is by and out of consciousness. Consciousness expresses as aspiration, aspiration as will, will as energy, energy as force, force as results. A manifestation of forms out of consciousness by the objectification of consciousness as form is the complete process of creation.

Process = Consciousness(Inherent Knowledge) -Aspiration-Will-Energy-Force-Results

Is it possible to convert the consciousness (inherent knowledge) into emotions and sensations that generate energy, force, results? Yes! The Impersonal Consciousness(knowledge) can be converted into personal power and results.

Knowledge is power. Complete knowledge is power to accomplish without negative consequences or side-effects. Such knowledge is unfailing. Accomplishment in life is about clarity, conviction, commitment, responsibility, determination, perseverance.

No task will come to you that is beyond your capacity to accomplish, if only you have the faith to accept it with that conviction.

Origin of achievement is in the INNER

All achievement originates inwardly, not outwardly. The outer success is the result of the right consciousness inside. Vision, aspiration, will, decision, commitment, right attitudes, right motives, high values, deep knowledge, inner strength, right perceptions of obstacles, harnessing the power of the spirit are among them. For all these, expanding energy is required in the inner.

Energy for the Expansion-Calling the 12 POWERS of SPIRIT

Any expansion requires great energy. In negative discipline, such as rejecting arising thoughts or suppressing selfish impulses, energy is consumed. Conversely, in positive discipline, energy is amplified. Instead of rejecting insistent thoughts, one can call in SILENCE. This approach is positive. We call in Silence for a greater result. It is mercenary. To call in Silence for Silence's sake is to be more positive. To call in Silence as a method is a finite act. To call in Silence because it is one aspect of the Spirit is to be Spiritual. **The twelve powers of the Spirit - Eternity, Infinity, Silence, Peace, Unity, Truth, Goodness, Knowledge, Power, Beauty, Joy and Love** - can thus be called in. It will expand the energy, enabling us to achieve our goals.

Strategy for continuous accomplishment by ever rising Aspiration, Inner Work and Shifting to Spirit

Being work-centric aims at results, while being centred on evolution focuses on the essence of life itself. Work itself is divine if we do not do it physically. To be centred in that WORK has a wider power of aspiration. As our aspiration quality rises, our energy expands endlessly. There is no end for it till one reaches Brahman (The Supreme Absolute.) In practice, one cannot raise his aspiration thus. In doing an experiment, one isolates himself from all activities and focuses on the work. Therefore the aspiration is intense. Suppose we do not focus like that, our energies are spread out all over our life activities. In such a condition no concentration is possible. For luck to become permanent and for continuous manifestation of our potentials and manifestation, the concentration must be there all the time. It is not easy. One way to handle that situation is to solve all the problems on hand using this Process and start availing of all the opportunities that present to us. One who does that will rise like A STAR. Certain attitudes acquired truly and permanently by INNER WORK help the process of CREATION AND ACCOMPLISHMENT.

A perfect sense of humility in all circumstances, adopting the Silent will and taking another man's point of view wherever possible, helps. If one can acquire it, it is a gateway to Supermind. Not to allow egoistic expression of any kind is very powerful but very difficult. Genuine goodwill to all is very powerful and it is possible for anyone to acquire it. Goodwill goes with generosity. As long as one sees the difference between generosity and vanity and shuns the latter, all qualities of which are mentioned above converge in GOODWILL embodying generosity.

Our whole concentration should be shifted from outer to inner and from downwards to upwards for attaining a resourceful state and for consistent accomplishments.

Success of our spirit manifests as success in our life. To know the secret of being successful does not lie in knowing what others have done or what strategies they have applied to be successful but rather what has driven them to do. To become successful, it is important for us to know what we have to do and not what others have done. Success is the outcome of integral existence of our life. Success in life mirrors success of the spirit.

Spirit is income. Life is an expenditure. Success will be ours as long as the Inner Spirit in us is more than life. ***The Spirit is the fuel of our life.*** When our Inner Spirit totally takes over life, unfailing success comes. It is like a genius taking an examination.

Consciousness-Knowledge-Will

Consciousness divides into Knowledge and Will.

Knowledge is the Light of the Consciousness.

Will is the Force of the Consciousness.

The more Will assimilates Knowledge, more the Will is integrated with Knowledge.

Building and Expanding Inner Capacities

Incapacity expects. Expectation postpones. Bridging the gap in capacity by capacity building, accomplishes.

Achieving this can be facilitated by following these steps:

1. **Awareness of Potential and Knowledge:** Recognise and understand the potential within oneself through acquiring knowledge.

2. **Expanding Attitude and Aspiration:** By expanding the attitude and aspiration, being selflessly eager for the prosperity of others and of the whole world.

3. **Increasing Faith in Spirit and Self-Confidence:** Develop greater faith in the spiritual dimension and confidence in one's own knowledge and abilities.

4. **Organising Energy for Progress:** Direct all energy towards upward growth and advancement rather than maintaining the status quo or dispersing it.

5. **Recognising Internal Determinants:** By discovering that the one and sole determinant is inside, not outside.

6. **Shifting Faith from Material to Spiritual:** Redirect faith from the value of money and material possessions to faith in the power of the Spirit and the internal determinant.

Accomplishment and the Sanction of One's Emotions

Here is another way of putting it. An individual may think about ways to improve himself, but that is not enough for achieving life's goals. One may even try, strive to accomplish something at a greater level, but that might not bring in the desired results. When the mind decides to accomplish, it needs the sanction of the vital, the emotions. The decision needs endorsement of our emotions to gain force and release energy. True force and purpose arise when there's a profound emotional desire to achieve. Attempting to accomplish solely through thought, devoid of emotional drive, will ultimately leave things as they are. When the sanction of the emotions is obtained, accomplishment of the thing gathers force, and attracts positive circumstance from life. This is the power of the emotions which releases the WILL AND FORCE and convert the KNOWLEDGE into RESULTS.

Unleashing the Power of Emotional Drive: A Man's Journey towards Wealth

Consider an individual desiring greater wealth. Despite this mental aspiration, emotionally they might feel content and secure in their current situation, perhaps valuing freedom over material gain. In such a case, their perceived need for more money won't translate into actual accumulation. Conversely, a profound hunger or ambition for wealth generates positive responses from life, drawing money towards them. Taking physical action aligned with this emotional drive completes the process, attracting wealth into their life. This holistic approach gathers the necessary force for accomplishment.

Ken Burns' Journey from Baseball to Jazz

While working on a film about baseball, filmmaker Ken Burns conceived of a film on the history of jazz. He thought it was a great idea and felt it would be an extension of his work on the baseball film. However, despite having the idea early on, he took no action on the jazz film for several years and could have started initial preparations while still working on the baseball film. It was only years later that he felt an **emotional stirring to pursue the jazz project**. From that moment, it came about very quickly, and with great intensity and organisation. Thus emotion energises and abridges time for accomplishment.

Overcoming Our Limitations

Take Inventory of Yourself as the First Step to Endless Progress. We are an amalgam of capacities and virtues. Each of us has exemplary, average, and weak parts of our nature and character. Throughout our lives, we succeed because of our strengths, but are held back because of our weaknesses. Human progress is often hindered by ego, ignorance, and superstition. True accomplishment comes from what is awakened within us.

Sample Wanting Attitudes that Block Achievement/ Response

1. PESSIMISM, INCAPACITY

"That is just too difficult"

"It's just too much to take on"

"It will never work out"

"It will take forever"

"There are no solutions for that"

"What's the use of trying"

"I can't do that"

"I don't have the energy for that"

"I can't do it all alone?"

2. RELUCTANCE

"I don't want to do that"

"I don't want to get involved"

"Let someone else take care of it"

"This is new; I cannot accept it"

"Leave me alone"

"I'll do it another time"

3. LIMITS

"5% growth is more than enough"

"The market is limited"

"There are limits to X"

"Let's play it safe"

"We only have limited funds"

"Resources are always tight"

"I must hold on to my money"

4. *OTHER PEOPLE*

"I'll have nothing to do with them"

"He's the cause of the problem"

"They'll just ruin things"

"They cannot be trusted"

"They're always trying to cheat me"

"They are impossible to control"

"They just won't cooperate"

"It's my way or the highway"

If one can consciously give up the wanting attitudes by inner work and embrace higher values and positive expansive attitudes, our inner and outer life flowers. Opening, sincerity, pleasantness, harmony, truth, efficient skill, finally perfect perfection when applied to any act will see it through. The capacity to evoke life responses at will gives one the power to accomplish anything in life. Then, regardless of the situation, the conditions, the apparent limitations, we can consciously attract the knowledge, the conditions and resources.

What we are doing subconsciously, we must aim to do consciously in our own lives. And to do it consciously means to progress much more quickly without the need for intense suffering as a spur to our awakening and effort.

Accomplishment results when internal and external conditions are positive (direction) and of sufficient intensity (strength). The matrix of four quadrants we saw in the chapter of Decision Making helps us in this process.

The objective is to enhance our capacity for accomplishment in life. The capacity for accomplishment in life is a direct function of our consciousness. The more conscious we are of life, the greater our knowledge of how human beings, organisations of people, social groups evolve, develop and accomplish in the wider plane of universal life.

The Process of Accomplishment: Vision, Direction, Organisation, Action(Manifestation)

To accomplish an ACT, one must know the **theory** by which the act is governed, the **principles** by which the act comes into existence, the **powers** it expresses in the planes of mind, vital and physical.

1. **Theory:** This refers to the fundamental principles that explain why the action is necessary and how it works. It's the "why" and "how" behind the action.

2. **Principles:** These are the guidelines that determine how the action comes into being. They define the steps and considerations involved in carrying out the action.

3. **Powers:** These are the ways the action manifests on different planes.

   a. *Powers in the mental plane are expressed by logic and rationality as arguments, explanations and examples.*

   b. *Powers in the vital plane are expressed as right human relationship, correspondence between events characterised by harmony and pleasantness.*

   c. *Powers in the physical plane involves the skills and abilities needed to handle the physical aspects of the action, including managing material resources, their interactions, and movements.*

In life, we often encounter consequences without fully understanding their underlying causes. We may remain **unaware of the process** behind them. However, gaining a comprehensive understanding of this process provides us with secret knowledge and a formula for altering both causes and consequences. This process is universal in nature.

The formula laid down here is applicable to any kind of act, whether small or big. All accomplishment starts from our Inner. It starts from the Vision.

Envision & Create Your Future

- Envision the goal you want to achieve
- Make sure it is clear in your mind
- Passionately desire for it to come about
- Make the decision & commitment to achieve it
- Organise the details, including right strategies
- Develop time bound to dos to make it happen
- Carry out your plan in a timely manner
- Make the full, determined effort
- Remain positive, optimistic, and enthusiastic
- Overcome corresponding wanting attitudes
- Execute your plan with the highest skills
- Focus on its attainment as exclusively as possible
- Aim to achieve the goal by your target date
- Open to the spiritual Force at every stage

Having dreams and visions alone is not enough for accomplishment. Having knowledge alone will not bring results. The three important ingredients to release the WILL and FORCE for Accomplishment are Direction, Organisation, Action.

1. Direction

- You become aware of the possibilities
- You narrow down the possibilities
- You envision what you want to accomplish
- Your emotions endorse it
- You make the decision to make it happen

2. *Organisation*

- You consider strategies to accomplish the goal
- You choose the best strategies
- You develop time bound actions to do, to make it happen

3. *Action*

- You execute to dos in a timely manner
- You execute with intensity, skill, and right attitudes

Life responds overwhelmingly!

The Infinite Power of Creation-Method of the Infinite

There is a process by which individuals create and accomplish in life. Interestingly, this process is not limited to acts we as individuals engage in, but **to all planes and fields of life** – whether it is a **business, family, social institutions, or society as whole.**

For example, when a business undertakes a strategic plan, it follows this same process from vision to decision to execution to manifestation. When followed diligently, meeting all of the conditions described earlier, the company not only achieves its goals, but also experiences powerful and positive life responses. The same is true for a family, a community, a nation, or any collective or aspect of society. When any entity rigorously follows these steps, it not only accomplishes what it intended, encountering instances of sudden good fortune.

Thus we observe that the process of creation is actually universal in nature, and applies to any aspect of life. In fact, that process also reflects how the universe itself originated from a divine Source. I.e. an Infinite consciousness conceived of a universe of forms of its own Force, and then organised and executed Its intent, bringing about the cosmos we know and live in. Thus, when we apply the process of creation and accomplishment in our own lives, **we are following the same essential method of the**

Infinite - from vision to direction to organisation to manifestation. And like that Divine Reality, we are **able to create infinite-like results in the very shortest period of time.**

Knowledge and Will Fused Enables Ultimate Accomplishment

Accomplishment is determined by the Knowledge we have and the Will to accomplish it. E.g., M can rise from project manager to project leader (Knowledge), and M intensely wants to make it happen (Will). When M makes the effort for it to occur, life cooperates, quickly bringing the object of M's desire. Conversely, if M has the knowledge without the will, or will without the knowledge, accomplishment will be difficult if not impossible. E.g., M knows how to rise from project manager to leader, but not the will to do it; or M have the will to rise to that level, but not the knowledge of how to do it. It's only when both Knowledge and Will converge, real accomplishment will be possible. Otherwise it remains as a distant dream. If M has both together, and then makes the persevering effort to bring it about, matched by high attitudes, then life will cooperate from all quarters. This integration is termed a Complete Act, which invariably prompts life to respond positively from all directions.

When we rise in consciousness, our knowledge of things and our will to accomplish it begin to fuse, our understanding of things and our determination to achieve them start to merge. This means that our rational thinking and our emotional drive begin to work together. In this state, we find harmony, and life tends to align with our endeavors. In other words, life responds positively to our efforts.

Sri Aurobindo refers to this state as "Truth Consciousness" or "Supermind," which represents the merging of Knowledge and Will. There is a complete, many-sided integral knowledge of a thing that is matched by a compulsion for its manifestation, accomplishment. This dual power is in fact how the universe came to be from a Divine source, and is something we can access in our own lives.

When we embrace the spiritual Force, we connect into Truth Consciousness, experiencing it as Truth Power. Through this connection, we gain not just comprehensive understanding but also the ability to manifest reality. Life responds as limitations of time and space fade away, allowing finite aspects to merge with the infinite. It is a way of living (and creating) that awaits humanity's future.

As we navigate our way through the steps of the Process of Accomplishment, we not only produce the expected practical outcomes but also encounter powerful, life-altering responses. In fact, the more perfectly we adhere to the process, the more likely and the greater the intensity of the response. On the other hand, if our effort lacks emotional spark, or is unfocused, haphazard, and disorganised, not only will we fail to achieve in a practical sense, but in a life response one as well.

This process is the most efficient means of manifesting your heart's desire and to evolve rapidly in life. This is the Spirit's method for rapid manifestation of your potentials for manifestation and accomplishment for a fulfilling life.

95

Bridging Psychological and Spiritual Gap

We can rapidly evolve our Being by consciously bridging the Psychological and Spiritual Gap.

Time differential in normal daily life

Our life is a constant state of becoming, moving from moment to moment. Whether we are bathing, dressing, eating, going to work, meeting clients, traveling on holiday, or attending a get-together, there is always a time differential between the present and the future activities we perceive and anticipate. We know it is a matter of time for that gap to be bridged. We see the unfolding of life events in its normal course. We all are aware of this time differential in our daily life.

Bridging the Psychological Gap

There is also another time differential between who we are now and who we can become in terms of our inner psychological landscape. Often, we are not keen to bridge this psychological gap because it requires changing our lower nature. Many of us are hardly, even aware of the gap in the first place. In fact, filling this gap is the main reason for our existence on earth and the evolutionary aim of this Creation and Existence. To evolve and grow in the Consciousness is the aim.

This gap and poverty consciousness can manifest as a negative attitude towards work, others, or life, as well as egotistical behaviour, anger, unwillingness to take up new opportunities, persistently late, laziness, impatience, intolerance of new ideas, etc. When we inwardly overcome these limiting attitudes, intents, habits, beliefs, opinions, and motives, life moves towards us with better conditions. For example, we might suddenly be offered a better-paying job, business may scale up, experience relief from chronic illness, a love longed for now, shows an interest from their side, a long-term conflict suddenly resolves itself, and so forth. This is a subtle phenomenon that operates beyond our usual boundaries of awareness, making the impossible possible. It reflects the subtle interplay of space and time, leading to transformative outcomes.

Becoming aware of our psychological deficiencies and reversing in our inner to bridge the gap by shedding the lower nature and embracing the higher values and consciousness, abridges the time of our evolution. By bridging the Psychological gap, we become future-ready and attract the future into our present life.

Steps to Bridge the Psychological Gap

1. **Recognise the Differential:** Acknowledge that a gap exists between your current self and your potential.

2. **Identify Deficiencies:** List out the specific deficiencies between what you are and what you can become.

3. **Take Action:** Make a deliberate effort to overcome at least one or two of these deficiencies.

4. **Be Sincere:** Ensure that your efforts to change are genuine and wholehearted.

5. **Experience Transformation:** Notice and embrace the sudden good fortune that comes your way as a result of making this concerted psychological effort.

In addition to bridging the psychological gap, we can also close the gap between our human selves and our spiritual selves. This path is not for everyone, but for those who feel an inner calling to pursue it.

Bridging the Spiritual Gap

Spiritually drawn individuals who are committed to personal evolution and transformation can attempt to bridge the spiritual gap and evolve their spiritual selves. A person may feel a deep desire to become more self-giving or to create a deep sense of calm within so that he can better meet the exigencies of life in future, to perform his daily activities using the vast spiritual force, etc This can involve performing daily activities with the support of vast spiritual forces. Each individual can create their own spiritual portfolio and aspire to bridge this gap.

For example, one person aspired to bring the spiritual Force into his life. He began by opening himself to his inner Spirit before engaging in activities and discovered that nearly every time, life responded with sudden good fortune. In this way, he has begun to bridge not only the psychological gap between his current and future self but also the spiritual gap.

96

Life Acts When an Individual Exerts and Exhausts Current Capabilities

Life, both in general and in particular, does not exhaust man's potential. Therefore, no problem created by that life is insurmountable for a higher inner power of man. There is always scope for us to exert ourselves to ascend higher.

We are not aware that we are exercising our choice every minute. The choice to exert or not. We take it as a way of life. There are literally thousands of occasions where one can witness two families - or individuals - of comparable circumstances at the end of thirty years of career separated by a vast social distance - one living cozily in a rural town enjoying the local social status and the other in Delhi or Washington riding the waves of social prestige in several fields. **It is made possible by the conscious exercise of choice at every minute.**

- The short term gain vs. long term benefit
- The occasion to exert vs. the least line of resistance
- The courage to embrace the new vs. the cozy comfort of tradition
- The readiness to risk vs. the sense of security, etc.

Those who prosper will look at the world from their highest responsibilities. Those who refuse to prosper will always attribute their failure to external circumstances. In the well-to-do families sometimes children decide

NOT to exert themselves and live by their existing resources or reputation. No man can exert himself for what he does not need. Generally, man left to himself, is unresponsive to development opportunities around him.

Doing One's Very Best: A Multidimensional Approach

To do one's very best can encompass several dimensions, sometimes involving all of them simultaneously:

1. **Exhausting Energy:**   Putting forth maximum physical and mental effort.

2. **Progression of Effort:**   Effort can be viewed on a scale from energy to results:

- Energy: The initial exertion of effort.

- Force: Energy directed by determination.

- Organisation: Structuring force into a coherent plan.

- Skill: Applying expertise to execute the plan.

- Result: The outcome of the organised effort.

In the progression of energy-force-organisation-skill-result, to exhaust one's energy is the least and easy. To try to exhaust one's force or organisation is more difficult. The higher one moves in the scale, the greater is the effort needed.

3. **Stages of Effort:**
- Aspiration to Will: Releasing willpower to initiate action.

- Will to Energy: Strength of will releases energy.

- Energy to Force: Energy becomes force with determination.

- Force to Power: Organising force into power through strong character.

- Power to Results: Power yields results based on available skill.

4. **Exhaustion Levels**:

- Energy: The basic level of effort.

- Determination: Higher level involving sustained focus.

- Character: Deeper level involving inner strength and integrity.

- Skill: Application of expertise for effective results.

So one can exhaust one's energy, determination, character, or skill.

5. **Higher Components**: Exhausting higher components like determination, character, and skill is more challenging and leads to greater accomplishments.

6. **Multilevel Effort**:   The very best may also be at several levels not only according to his endowments, but also according to his willingness to exert.

Spirit and life operate in a million dimensions, reflecting the complexity and depth of human endeavor. We can make life respond by exerting and exhausting our current capabilities.

Overcoming Project Bottlenecks: The Power of Persistent Effort

Often in the course of a project, progress grinds to a halt due to bottlenecks. There may be a need for new ideas, new information, more men, money, materials, etc. At these times, it's beneficial to step back and examine the overall functioning of the institution in the light of the principles already described.

When the atmosphere surrounding the work is unfavourable and disharmony prevails, it is wise to patiently refrain from action and observe. However, when the atmosphere is positive and all elements seem ready for a breakthrough, even a token effort may turn the corner and bring success. This involves making a determined initiation and persistent endeavor, no matter how small, and exhausting all possibilities, potentials, and resources available.

At the point where one has fully exhausted their energies and capacities, life responds by providing the necessary components to complete the work. When human effort is fully expended, one opens up to the forces of universal life, which then take up the movement. However, if one stops just before the final step, there is no response.

The Challenge of Sustaining Positive Change by continuous exertion

We see many lives of the individuals. A certain way of life led them to a dead end. Few who are fortunate, by grace, endeavour to change themselves to get over from the dead end by invoking the higher power in their life. This brings about a dramatic change in their dire situation, alleviating all their difficulties for the moment. However, as soon as they find relief, they revert to their old habits that initially caused their problems, such as anger, stinginess, clumsiness, assertion, deceit, and lying. Their complaints grow even louder: "My Lord, what a predicament I am in. Why is life so cruel to me?" Life is not cruel to them; they simply refuse to exert and learn. Instead, they stubbornly return to the behaviours that ruined them. Life, Force, Spirit, wait patiently for them to learn on their own. The saying "you can lead a horse to water, but you can't make it drink" is very true in this context.

One must be drawn to the Spirit, the spiritual aspect of any part of the being to constantly exert himself in invoking the Spirit which will make his life a marvel.

97

Reversal of the past errors

All our problems arise out of the arrears in the past. It exists as mental arrears. It is a way of accumulation of karma due to unconsciousness and ignorance. All our past errors wait for consecration. Consecration has power to dissolve the Karma and the mental arrears. Reversal of past errors and consecrating dissolves the unconsciousness and as knowledge lights up from within and consciousness grows, it is a way to avoid emergence of future problems of the same type. It is a profound way of learning from experience instead of repeating past errors.

To correct the errors of sense-mind by pure reason is a chief instrument of man. Transcendent can arrive in us through pure reason, says Sri Aurobindo. There are various layers. Reason and logic is the first step and involves mental and intellectual aspects. Going further deep, consciousness replaces thoughts and imparts a much wider understanding of aspects of our self and life.

"Past consecration" lends itself to a deep sense of "apology" for past errors, contrition and within oneself. It also gives the knowledge of the cause of the errors and the ignorance dissolves.

Learning from the Past to Improve Your Present

Our past negatives are the cause of our current problems. By taking time for quiet reflection, you can identify the negative thoughts, beliefs, or actions that led to your current situation. Owning these mistakes and acknowledging them with sincerity allows you to release them and seek

168

guidance from a higher power (the Spirit) for positive change. This process can open doors to solutions and attract circumstances that resolve the problem, leading to a brighter future.

In us there are arrears in the Mind. Most of them we will know. Whatever we do not know, meditation will reveal. Consecrating your past errors in deed and consciousness to Spirit, you will quickly attract enormous benefit into your life in the near future. This powerful spiritual method is called "Past Consecration." It is acknowledging and releasing those past mistakes (both what you did and what you thought) to a higher power. For us time exists as past, present and future. But in truth, Time exists as one continuous stream wherein past, present and future exists together and thus each can influence the other. Thought expresses the past in terms of the future in the present. Reversal of past changes the present and future. All successions of the past are included in the present which is the beginning of the future.

At each point where you shift from a wanting element of your consciousness to its positive equivalent, there will be a positive life response.

People will happily jump to quick judgement and conclusions even without all the information in hand. They then look completely foolish in retrospect.

If you regret something you discarded for good reason, it will suddenly begin to come back! It's important to learn from past experiences and move forward. Many people constantly dwell in the past without conscious reversal of the past and they remain stagnant or worsen themselves and their current situations.

If you learn the lessons failure has provided, life will lift you to the heights.
Failure to learn from past failures will keep you in the same place, or worse. If one feels intense contrition for a serious mistake, a solution that resolves it tends to well-up from life.

Consecrate to activate your Inner Power centre of Knowingness

One who knows ALL the rules of accomplishment is not guaranteed success as knowing is not doing. If the knowing is intellectual, it is to know in the outside. When the knowing is an insight or intuition, it is to know inside. A previous experience shifts the outer knowing to the inner knowledge. Previous experience even when unpleasant and a failure can act as a solid foundation for us to gain wisdom through the power of inner knowingness and consecration serve as a tool to access to our inner power of knowingness. A powerful shift happens when intellectual knowledge transforms into intuitive knowledge. This can be triggered by a past experience that bridges the gap between "knowing" and "doing."

A conscious inner process of education and conscious evolution begins with consecration of each of the past failures until it resolves into equality. By bringing the memory of the past to the present, the mind is educated not to repeat the old errors. **Psychologically it is known as humility, spiritually as sincerity, evolutionarily it is known as knowledge emerging from Ignorance.**

Contrition for Ego-Based Negative Undoes the Result

Feeling sincere remorse (contrition) and setting free (consecrating) an Ego-oriented action that attracts a negative, can reverse the negative consequences. This act of acknowledging your mistake and letting it go helps move things back in the right direction.

The Pitfall of Greed: A Website's Story

A website owner was doing well with online advertising. His income was steadily increasing. However, greed took hold. He wanted even more and sought advice on maximising his earnings. Unfortunately, shortly after, his website took a hit. Viewership and income dropped by 25% or more —the reverse of what he intended. Reflecting on his actions, he realised his mistake. He understood that his initial success was due to organic growth, and he understood his greedy, ego-oriented action and unnecessary initiative disrupted the positive flow. Feeling remorse, he acknowledged his mistake to a higher power (spiritual Force) and then let it go. He stopped obsessing over the situation and focused on maintaining the quality of his website.

The good news? The website soon recovered everything it lost. Traffic and income returned to their previous levels, and the website continued to grow steadily, this time without the pressure of forced expansion.

Consecration of Past errors and failures cures negative consequences of Over-expectation

When Opportunity Knocks, Don't Let Expectation Spoil It.

Imagine a poor person suddenly presented with a life-changing opportunity. Instead of joy, they become burdened by fear and expectation. They worry that this chance might be ruined, which ironically increases the likelihood of it happening. The energy released due to Over-expectation spoils the opportunity. The problem is, completely eliminating expectation is impossible. Here's the key:

1. ***Let Go of Past Failures***:   Instead of trying to erase expectation altogether, focus on letting go of past mistakes and anxieties. By consecrating these burdens, you free yourself from the negative patterns that fuel excessive expectation.

2. ***Consecration Creates Space***:   When you release the baggage of the past, you create space for a more positive outlook. This allows you to approach the opportunity with openness and appreciation, maximising your chances of success.

Consecration dissolves expectation when the past errors and failures are consecrated.

Three Keys to Accomplishment

Three things are necessary for any accomplishment.

1. **Positive Mindset:** You need a positive capacity for creation and to accomplish something.

2. **Avoid Negativity:** Dwelling on negativity hinders success. It cancels luck.

3. **Correcting Past Mistakes:** you must have the capacity to compensate for your earlier errors, omissions, false steps and wrong actions and make amends. This is referred to as "reversing your karma" through consecration.

Clearing the Path to Success

True accomplishment requires addressing all the negatives of the past. No accomplishment is possible until all the errors, misconceptions, tricks, and false steps are withdrawn or eliminated.

98

Transformation

The Path to Transformation: Developing Consciousness

The consciousness through which we see ourselves determines the consciousness through which others see us. Our self-perception has a powerful effect on how others see us. If we view ourselves with confidence and positivity, it radiates outward.

If we want to rapidly evolve and self-transform ourselves, we have to grow conscious. Development of consciousness is the key for transformation.

Development of consciousness leads to all round development. Transformation occurs through knowledge, assimilation and realisation.

Transformation through Higher Values

Developing our consciousness to adopt higher values will spur our material and social development. Our capacity for progress, both as individuals and societies, is directly linked to our level of consciousness. Human choice and capacity are the ultimate determinants of progress.

As society has evolved and acquired values through prolonged development, it can now advance further by consciously adopting higher values. This principle also applies to individuals. Values bring out the hidden potentials. Present potentials are clues to future realisation..

Every time we create a new thought, new idea, we reincarnate in our life. Old ways will not open new doors. We have to constantly reorient, reinvent and reincarnate ourselves each moment for constant evolution and transformation by embracing higher values.

The Influence of Receptivity and Inner Transformation on Our Circumstances

Our level of receptivity has a great influence on our circumstances. Our present situation, position, and poise determine what can come to us. Our willingness to receive determines what comes to us. Our unwillingness prevents other things from coming.

When we grieve that something is not coming to us, it stems from aspiring for something for which we are unwilling to create receptivity. Feeling frustrated that something hasn't happened often stems from wanting it without being truly prepared for it. Only aspiration is not enough. It has to be accompanied by willingness to receive. We need to do the inner work and transform ourselves to create the right conditions for what we aspire.

Saying "I am good" sets a boundary on our goodness. True goodness requires the strength to be limitless goodness.

- For honesty, amount is the limit.
- For conduct, the situation is the limit.
- For selfishness, pride and comforts are the limits.
- For magnanimity, prestige is the limit.

We often comfort ourselves by believing that everything has limits. While some limitations imposed by situations or goodness are necessary, the limits that arise from our capacity to be good are unwelcome. There are no limits for our capacity to be supremely good and to express limitless goodness.

While having good qualities is a good start, it's not enough for true conscious evolution and transformation. We can rise higher due to any potential and make it permanent. Rising higher in a moment is one thing, but making it permanent is another. When we are not disturbed, we can rise on the strength of one or more potentials. In order to rise permanently and to constantly evolve, negative traits must be eliminated. True growth involves not just cultivating good qualities but also actively working to overcome negative traits.

The Inner Reflects the Outer: Understanding Life's Truism

As you are inside, so you are outside. This is a fundamental truth of life. God is Infinite and Eternal, perhaps even a ZERO, while we are finite. What we perceive as God is merely our interpretation of God. According to the Gita, one can become anything through sincere aspiration. In other words, we are today what we subconsciously aspired to be in the past. This can be difficult to accept for many. A beggar may ask if he aspired to become a beggar. One who has become bankrupt can ask if he aspired for bankruptcy. Spiritually, however, this holds true. A soul who was a king in a previous life may choose to be born as a beggar in the next life to experience different aspects of existence and further its evolution. Someone who seeks to understand the true meaning and value of wealth subconsciously knows that he will get that knowledge only when he tastes bankruptcy. Thus, he 'courts' bankruptcy. This is often confirmed by the fact that subsequent generations of a bankrupt person frequently find themselves ushered into wealth. Thus, *our current circumstances can be seen as part of a larger spiritual journey, embracing diverse experiences for growth and transformation.* Transformation and accomplishment in this world is discovering the true reality of existence and spirit in life and to evolve in the universal rhythm of our existence and life.

Cosmic Dance of Evolutionary Transformation:From Ego to Soul

The true source of conflict is within whether it is individual or society or nation.

The real Adversary is Ego. Fear, jealousy, insecurity, and selfishness are just a few ways our "ego" manifests. It creates the illusion of being separate and alone in a vast universe. It gives a feeling of living isolated, unconnected and helpless in an oceanic universe struggling every moment to survive against and even at the expense of others, to carve out for oneself some safe territory and modicum of security, to acquire the power to protect oneself, which could only be done by dominating over those around. It is ego that urges one to seek the sense of enjoyment that issues from being more important and successful than others, demonstrating one's superiority, demonstrating superiority, having more, achieving more, knowing more than others.

The problem is inside us, not in others. The ego of other people come to act and impinge upon us only in the measure that we live in and assert our own ego.

Life is only a cosmic dance of Spirit seeking to manifest itself in an evolutionary progression through transformation. Every dancer requires a partner. Then how could the One dance? It could dance by becoming the Many and orchestrating the movements of each of its million selves to precisely coordinate with those of each of the others in order to at all times maintain the harmony of the underlying oneness, no matter how rapid, complex and violent the movement of its steps. Our ego-driven interactions create a chaotic version of this cosmic dance- – a reflection of our internal disharmony. Our ego participates in a cosmic dance of all the egos with whom we come in contact–offending, dominating, colliding, bruising, hurting, submitting, regretting and rejoicing successively and sometimes simultaneously–until the ego gives way to the infinite expansiveness of spiritual individuality, allowing the soul to come forward for a more divine dance of soul with soul.

Just as with individuals, tribes, classes, castes, and nations have their own narrow, egoistic identities that they struggle to maintain and assert against others. They too participate in the cosmic dance, bumping up against each other, pushing, shoving, rising, falling, hurting and being hurt. They aggrandise themselves at the expense of others, only to eventually serve as fodder for the self-aggrandisement of their former serfs, slaves, and subordinates. In this dynamic, one can perceive the cosmic mechanism at work, orchestrating movements for the progress of each and the evolution of all.

Perceiving Inner-Outer Correspondence for Transformation

Every problem has a solution, and the solution to every problem lies within the problem itself and the problem always lies in us. The human tendency is always to discover the problem in others, to project it on our adversaries. That was the real problem. If life is a perfectly orchestrated cosmic dance then every problem that we encounter from others might actually reflect a corresponding element in our own nature, either something of the past that needs to be transformed or something of the future that needs to be born. In either case it requires a pressure and a circumstance to help in that transformation or that new birthing. The very transformation is a new birthing itself.

God created the sense of sin so that human beings could grow aware of the limitations in their own consciousness and overcome them. Man outsmarted God. He has employed that capacity to discover the sins in others, rather than knowing the sins within himself.

The Key to Solving Problems lies in Self-Change. The solution to any problem lies not in changing others or waiting for them to change, but in changing the corresponding element within oneself that attracted, created, sanctioned, or necessitated the problem in the first place. For every external force, influence or event that impinges on our lives, there must be a corresponding inner supporting element. The solution is to find and reverse that internal element, not to change other people.

If others are adamant or insistent, defensive or aggressive, selfish or blind, impatient or intolerant, those characteristics could not impact our lives and consciousness unless there was a corresponding element within ourselves. What comes from outside comes with a mission and a purpose—regardless of the conscious intention that motivates others. It comes to liberate us from our own limitations and help us become more perfect in our consciousness. That is the knowledge needed to solve any problem of any type on any scale. When this knowledge is consciously applied, one can see that this knowledge has the power to achieve in an instant what might otherwise take years, lifetimes, or generations to accomplish.

Without an inner corresponding element, even the tiniest problem could not exist. If even a tiny problem existed that wasn't caused by our own limitations, it would throw the entire order of the universe into question. It would suggest that the world is maya, an illusion, or worse, a hell or purgatory where what happens to us is unrelated to who we are and what we can become. This perspective turns the world into an existential nightmare of meaninglessness, a real chaos or quantum world.

However, the world is not an illusion, hell, or nightmare. It is a progressively unfolding miracle and marvel.

Prosperity through Spiritual Transformation

When one moves from poverty to prosperity, the grip of religion, particularly orthodoxy and fundamentalism, generally weakens. Prosperity loosening the grip of religion opens to greater knowledge through education and paving the way for spirituality. Spirituality is the essence, whereas religion is merely a cover layer.

The best foundation for spirituality is prosperity. Spirituality is fulfilled in the material plane through wealth, new technologies, new possibilities, and the application of spirit to the details of life. Low income, poverty, religion, prosperity, education, knowledge, spirituality, and divinisation of life represent several progressive stages. The order can vary depending on time and place.

Spirituality culminates in the divinisation of life on earth, including the emergence of a new divine-like species. Evolution of consciousness followed by evolution of the substance, the physical substance of the body, transforming into a body of light manifesting the spirit in the cells is the next species going to dawn, after Man. (Supramental Species through transformed divinised body).

Note to Readers-Discover the Path to Self-Evolution and Transformation

Readers interested in consciously self-evolving for rapid transformation, expanding their consciousness, transforming their body, enhancing energy levels, curing diseases, or rejuvenating their body, may find valuable insights in my two books. These books contain 12,221 prayers, which are prayers of the cells: *Prayers of the Body for Divine Life, Volume 1: 5555 Prayers* and *Volume 2: 6666 Prayers*. Both volumes are available on Amazon.

99

Moving Life from Within, Secret Knowledge for New way of living

A New Dawn: Embracing a Different Way of Living

We've come a long way together. We've explored remarkable stories where life reacted in unexpected and powerful ways. We've delved into the reasons behind these phenomena – understanding the subtle workings of life and the inner and outer human behaviours that trigger the life responses.

And yet as we go through these experiences, we are likely to notice something else taking shape in our inner journey. We might be standing on the verge of a completely new kind of human existence – something unlike anything we've ever seen before. ***It is a new way of being, a new way of living born out of new consciousness.*** It is a rebirth in this very life. We start to Move Life from Within as a Harbinger of New Way of Living.

Life Response: A New Way of Living

Life response is not just a phenomenon that dazzles or miraculous occurrences leading to success; it serves as an indicator of a new form of existence—a fresh human functionality radically different from anything that has come before.

For countless millennia, we believed that by navigating life's challenges and meeting its conditions, and embracing its challenges, we would receive our fair share. In this view, life itself is the determinant, and we are mere respondents trying to make our way in the world. Whereas in this new reality, our perceptions are reversed. We shift from the determinism of the outer world to that of the inner. Here, in this new life, we become the creators of our world, setting its conditions and directing its course from within. Consequently, life constantly moves in our favour.

In this new reality, the equation of life is reversed, as positive conditions gravitate towards us on their own, without any effort on our part. We do not seek out life; instead, life seeks us out. Life constantly moves towards us from out of nowhere. This is the hallmark of a new way of living.

The Way of Future Individual-A Spiritual Individual

Traditionally, we achieve our goals by developing a strong intention and then acting on it. This method of inner intention followed by outer activity has been instinctively practiced for thousands of generations. And yet this approach may not be the preferred approach in the future – especially for a potential group of emerging individuals. These individuals will no longer be guided by external social influences but will instead be oriented inwardly as Spiritual Individuals.

The Future Individual will move life from within, harnessing vast inner powers and significantly reducing the amount of outer action required to achieve results. Moreover, the outer results that do come from this inner orientation and approach will unfold miraculously—suddenly and abundantly.

Individuals with an inner orientation have been known to evoke miraculous results—such as suddenly ending an energy crisis or resolving conflicts and wars. Once we experience achieving without moving a muscle or communicating a thought, we begin to see life differently. The world then appears as an endless opportunity, instantaneously accessible from within. At that point, we will have taken a decisive step toward a very different kind of existence—A "New Way of Living."

How this New Way of Living look like?

Life will be smooth, serene, spontaneous, and dynamic. In this reality, life is not only abundant but fully cooperative, with all conditions under one's control. In this existence, one not only experience a continuous stream of good fortune but also feels a deep, abiding joy and delight in living. Life will be not ordinary with struggle but an extraordinary one that each of us can experience on our own.

The essential question that remains is: Are you prepared to change your ways; to reorient your life; to turn the inner keys that will enable you to live in this New Consciousness. If you are, then you are welcome to this New Dawn and New Way of Living. After millennia of struggle, it is purely a Divine Grace that this WISDOM is given to us and the ATMOSPHERE is ripe for us to embrace this WISDOM and EVOLVE IN JOY AND HARMONY. The time has come for evolution to change its nature. The evolution which happened in struggle and ignorance changes into evolution in joy and wisdom.

The Secret Knowledge

Having this secret knowledge of Inner-Outer Correspondence and Subtle-Truths of Life, our revolution is replaced by evolution, due to our inner transformation.

Shifting to our inner, further going to the depths, gaining capacity to remain in the depths and to live our life from the depths is a great path for rapid evolution.

Evolved human consciousness that knows Reality and its subtle life laws can move the life from within. Everything around us are expressions of the multiplicity of the One and the One Spirit.

- The Secret Knowledge is to perceive spirit and life integrally entangled, comprising the Reality.

- The Secret Knowledge is to perceive the spirit unfolding in life, furthering the evolution.
- The Secret Knowledge is to have the wisdom of the nature of Reality, the All, and know the means of furthering evolution, enabling the infinite to arise from the finite in life.

Through our higher consciousness we continuously perceive the right relation and deeper truth of things. We reconcile contradictory forces, opposites in our lives; living naturally, harmoniously.

Our perception of evil persists as long as we rely on it to navigate through the egoistic ignorance in which we are involved. In other words, evil is not merely an unpleasant experience to endure or a fault of God. It serves as a Divine instrument to guide us in uncovering our own divinity. Once we grasp this understanding, once we acknowledge it, once we comprehend the purpose behind the influence of evil on our lives, we gain the ability to eliminate it—not by fighting on God's side but by becoming God in our own consciousness.

To summarise, the evil that comes to us from outside -only appears as such to our ego-driven consciousness that needs to make progress and needs evil as a mirror to help it make that progress. This is not new knowledge to the world. It was succinctly expressed over two thousand years ago in this passage from ancient Tamil Sangam literature:

"Good and evil do not come to you from outside."

When we internalise this knowledge not merely as a mental or intellectual formula–but when we are able to perceive the truth of it in our own lives, there remains just one more stride to conquer. We simply need to look beyond the appearance of evil, look behind the horrible and ferocious veil, and we will discover the Marvel waiting to reveal itself. As we accomplish this, we realise that the abhorrence, horror, and detestability we once associated with it simply vanish. Whether this disappearance occurs solely within our personal lives or extends to a broader scope of human existence depends on the power of personal consciousness we have acquired, a power that is progressively enhanced each time we succeed in this attempt. Then we discover that there is no ultimate sanction for evil in the universe, except for our attachment to it.

Discovering the secret of life requires objectivity, insight, sincerity, vision, and above all, courage—particularly courage. Those who possess the courage to look within themselves and search for the sources of the inner darkness that generate the need for the evil that comes to them from outside are qualified for this secret knowledge. Conversely, those who persist in blaming others, the world, life, or God for their sufferings, as well as those of their fellow human beings, may find this explanation unsatisfying. It is extremely difficult to look upon the external appearance of things without concluding that something is terribly wrong with the world, and since few individuals possess the insight to see deeply within or to grasp the wider evolutionary movement, any accusations may appear justified. However, this understanding provides a key for those who seek to eradicate evil from their own consciousness and life.

100

Relationship in married life

Marriage is a sacred union that requires dedication, understanding, and mutual respect to thrive. In today's fast-paced world, maintaining harmony in marriage has become more crucial than ever. All problems in marriage arise out of the attitude of <u>taking undue advantage over another</u>. Let us delve into the essential principles that can guide couples towards a fulfilling and enriching relationship.

This chapter is based on an article by Sri Karmayogi about the husband-wife relationship, originally written in Tamil, as well as some of his other writings. He offers profound insights into this highly challenging relationship, which I believe will greatly benefit readers by helping them understand the dynamics involved. Readers are encouraged to share these enlightening insights with their children and others who may find them beneficial.

Conflict is a natural and healthy component of all human relationships. The role of conflict, especially in married relationships, is very high. It is wise to ponder and reflect as most of the readers have shared experiences of married life, which are common, unlike the less frequent spiritual experiences.

In human relationships, absence of tension is not enough. We don't choose our marriage partners just because they never make us tense. Such a choice is based on a negative concept. Instead, we choose our partners because of the positive dynamics created by complementary and in some ways contradictory personalities. This interplay is the source of the energy, vitality, charm, attraction, and delight that lies at the heart of human relationships.

Man's deep attraction towards Woman

The greatest of contradictions is that between Man and Woman. When this contradiction evolves into complementarity, it naturally produces the greatest results from the greatest contradictions. This is why Man is so deeply attracted to Women. Contradictions offer greater fulfillment than complements when approached with the transformative attitude of converting them into complements. On this scale, family happiness is low and romance is at the peak. Of all the phenomena of life, woman presents the greatest contradiction to man, and thus, the greatest fulfillment.

The Unique Fulfillment of the Man-Woman Relationship

The one who by his soul accepts the God through deep meditation gets into state of trance. The sleep that comes seeking is due to ripening of sweet feelings through mind in intimate marriage life. Even though friendship has this attainment, where there is no gender difference, natural fulfillment ceases with feeling. Only man-woman relationship can fulfill a relationship between two people.

Various Stages of Union in Husband Wife Relationship- (Physical-Vital-Mental-Soul)

Marriage and childbirth is the first stage of union. It is applicable to animals as well. Human life differs from animal life only by wisdom. Second stage of union is union of life with another life in heart centre (vital-feelings). This we call it as ONE LIFE (in two bodies). There is little chance for union of mind with another mind in marriage life, although it is possible. Marriage life is confined to daily needs and customs of the society. Although husband and wife may have intelligent thoughts, these do not play a significant role in marriage. The next stage of union is at the soul level. Since the soul's journey is individual, the union of souls in marriage does not occur.

Though husband and wife completing their material life in the first stage is the worldly practice, those who are united in bodies, can unite by feelings. It happens. Further, union can be attained at the level of mind, after going from the first stage to the next stage of feelings, feelings fulfill the body. If it happens, the union in the first stage will give fulfillment in the second stage. If the husband gets a small injury while shaving in the morning, the wife at the next room comes fast with panic in heart. This is the union at level of feelings.

Personality in our home

We are capable of mentally overcoming the causes of daily frustrations. We do not take the effort to overcome our despair by the sober knowledge of the mind. We let our emotions get the better of us instead of thinking things through calmly. We indulge in our frustrations and grow morally indignant, "How can I be slighted in my own house? Is she a woman? Are they children? Do they behave like children? Have I not sacrificed my all for these very ungrateful people?"

One may be entirely right or entirely wrong. But this attitude has not yielded joy for anyone. What can one do? Perfection and imperfection co-exist. If you can see perfection fully in all its details, imperfection disappears. Try to see only the good side of others. Discipline yourself to see ONLY the good side of all the others, how much they inwardly endeavour to please you, to accommodate with your temperament, to rise to the great occasion of your idiosyncrasies, your extraordinarily inflated EGO, your inordinate ambition, your impossible temperament, etc. That will unleash the deeper GOOD side of yours which is all full of emotional appreciation for everyone, the GOOD ANGEL in you. It is worth trying at least once. If you ever succeed, don't be lost in your innate, inherent goodness! Try to learn the LAW there.

Difference between Life problems and Marriage problems

Usually marriage problems are life problems. Life problems are wider and include marriage problems.

- **Domination**:   Marriage has its own problems. Chief among them is the desire to dominate others. Harmony is the principle and happiness is the sensation. Absence of the motive to dominate the other is the eternal source of everlasting happiness. Domination embodies an egoistic mindset, which is increasingly frowned upon in both public and private spheres across all levels of organisations. The man dominates physically and compensates for that by submitting psychologically to his wife. The motive for dominating can be raised to one of love. Domination deteriorating into mean tyranny degenerates. To submit out of love and to take liberties makes marriage alive.

- **Money, caste, honor, give-and-take, age, property** are problematic in life. If they come into marriage, they are not marriage problems but life problems.

- Marriage is an arrangement of the society.

- **Civilisation, culture** of the country determines the social law. They also determine marriage problems.

- **Expectation**:   The basis of the problem is our motive to have others to be as we want. The root of many problems often lies in our desire for others to conform to our expectations.

- **Adaptability**:   It is Civility that we adapt ourselves to others. Civility is demonstrated by our willingness to adjust ourselves to accommodate others. When one accepts the other and adjusts as per the needs of other partner in married life, it prevents many problems from arising.

- **Unfit person**:   Person unfit to live is also unfit for marriage. If the problem arose by an unfit person getting married, it is not a marital problem but the life problem of the person who is unfit to live.

- **Culture difference**: When a highly cultured family arranges a marriage alliance with one of lower cultural standing, the problem that arises is the problem of lack of culture and not a marriage problem.

- The foundation of marriage, as well as life itself, rests on factors such as health, income, and good habits. The problem arising due to **deficiency of health, income, and good habits** is not a marital problem but a life problem.

- The matrimonial **relationship cannot be easily broken** like breakup in any other relationship, for example -friendship. The challenges that emerge within marriages are specifically categorised as marriage problems.

- Since marriage is an inescapable relationship, there's plenty of room for demands. When **demanding, if forced beyond the limit,** it becomes an insoluble problem.

- Life problems are **problems of Character (Gunas)**. Character is embedded deep behind manners, behaviours. Lack of character arises due to lack of culture in the behaviour and acts. (From a deeper perspective, the roots of one's character lies in one's values, beliefs.) If this is removed, then the marriage problems are negligible.

- Most marital problems are problems caused by **deliberate attempts to create trouble** and gain from it.

- The reason why problems are slightly more in **new relationships, inter-caste marriage**, is not because of marriage but because of other reasons.

- If husband and wife have 10 problems, 7, 8 of them are caused by **other family members.**

- Whether it is a woman or a man, **new habits** will invariably emerge after marriage. It cannot be known beforehand.

- If unavoidable situations arise, instead of having an accepting **mentality**, if one tries to avoid such situations, then the marriage will break down.

- At times **parents** try to create problems and spoil the lives of couples.

- **Temperament:** The problems caused by an unloving husband and an unaffectionate mother-in-law by nature are not marital, they are due to temperamental nature. Problems will arise even if there is no marriage.

- Status difference: The difficulties faced by rich girl after getting married and living in a poor family is one which arises from status difference, not of marriage.

- A boy who grew up in poverty, after he became well -off, not allowed his wife to eat was a problem due to **poverty consciousness** and not of marriage.

- **Attraction towards other**: When the mind is attracted to the other person, the marriage dissolves. The gap created in the relationship appears hollow. Marriage fragrance goes away. 'Marriage' will die if the mind is fond of another person.

- More than half of the marriages have no problems. **Creating troubles wantedly** is an unforgivable offence.

- There is nothing sweeter feeling to masculine than femininity.

- The mind seeks charm defying its thousand obscenities. The **mind cannot seek Character**. Only Soul seeks character.

- **Chastity**: A woman's pure chastity is the ability to invoke God without doing penance and yoga. Even the God of Time is bound by the solidity of chastity. Purity of mind in a wife ensures the longevity of the husband.

- Marriage is the **embryo of the family**.

- The first condition to be a good spouse is that one should be **aware of all one's faults.**

- One cannot eradicate all faults at once. An attitude of **not insisting on faults** is essential. While in action, it requires a mindset that struggles against its faults.

- **Refusing to see the faults of others** is as important as not emphasising one's own faults.

- One should **associate only with other's perfections** so as **not to be affected by the shortcomings of others.**

- We should **accept others as we accept ourselves.** The husband should accept the wife, the wife must accept the husband in the same way. Harmony arises from this mutual acceptance.

- **Peace** is the basis of a prosperous life.

- **Higher Enjoyment**:   He who achieves in life is the one who enjoys life. Life can be enjoyed in a higher way and in a lower way. A person who enjoys married life in the highest way will achieve more in life.

- A person who seeks **success in marriage** should achieve well in life.

- **The greater the freedom, the greater the achievement.**

- Giving freedom to others increases one's achievement.

- The **freedom given to the couple** within the limits of their strength determines the pinnacle of **achievement in married life.**

- If the couple's fault is not emphasised then the marriage will be successful. A person who wants to give Yogic conditions for marriage should accept the fault of the couple as his fault.

- **Subconscious attracts**:   A wife, who does not lie, if she gets a husband who can only lie, must accept that her consciousness is a lie deep down. The faults seen in the other visibly are the faults hidden in oneself in the subconscious. As the wife, though on appearance not tell lies but in her subconscious, has the capability to tell lies, she attracts a husband who can only lie. The deficiencies seen in others are actually the deficiencies of the one who sees the deficiencies. Life brings persons in our life to help us get rid of our deficiencies and evolve by this method.

- A **petty husband** does not like a responsible, superior wife. A wife who is childish, immature and small-minded will be delicious to him.

- **Childish couples** though often fight, they remain mutually supportive and passionate.

- **Ordinary couples**, **speaking openly**, can raise problems that do not exist. When a person while speaking openly, told about his own faults and the other person later when points out these faults, the division which happens during that time, does not disappear later.

- **Affectionate couples** do not necessarily have to be good or superior. Only affection is enough, others can be complete or partial.

- Husband and wife are basically rivals.

- **Conflict of family superiority**: The fundamental issue is whose family is superior.

- Both families trying to prove that they are inferior by marriage is the **seed of competition and fight.**

- The husband wants his wife should follow his word. The wife wants the husband to follow her word. Both are wrong. It is right and wise to be nice, honest, sweet and delicious.

- **Suspicion** can mentally end married life. A person with faults, is suspicious of others. It is foolish to behave in a manner that arouses suspicion when there is no reason for it. Once suspicion arises, it will not go away.

- **Not see the Shortcomings**: It is one condition that the other person should not see his shortcomings. Another condition is to praise oneself in spite of one's shortcomings.

- **Generosity in Appreciation**: A successful marriage is ensured by the ability to recognise and generously honor one's spouse's endowments.

- **Fulfillment in family**: Family should be full of fragrance for married life to be fragrant. There can be no fulfillment in marriage without fulfillment in family and community.

- **Trying to fulfill one's unfulfilled desire through the other**: It is common for both men and women to try to accomplish through their spouse, something which has not happened in their lives. Usually it is a false right. This attitude is the beginning of conflict.

- **Imposing on the other**: It is not proper for a couple to impose anything on each other. Lack of character is the cause of all conflicts that arise. Selfishness is the root cause of all disputes.

- **Ideal marriage, Ideal couple:** An Indian genius wrote, except in the pages of fiction there is no ideal marriage. The reality is that the ideal couple is real in the fantasy world.

- **Closed mouth of argumentative wife gaining Husband's Adoration:** A beautiful girl who used to argue always, after marriage, decided not to argue. The old lady professor who knew her said, 'You do not know how much your husband adores and idolises you.' All his devotion and worship is for her closed mouth. If she opens mouth, one can perform asceticism without thinking.

- **To treat the spouse equally**: One is submissive or dominant and cannot treat the other equally. It is human nature. Treating equally requires mental control.

- **Balancing Power in Marriage, Submission out of love for a Vibrant and Fulfilling Relationship:** If power is not exercised, the marriage will lose its liveliness. That is what a woman is looking for in man. Power shown extremely, when it becomes too alkaline, there won't be liveliness. When a man exerts too much control or dominance, it can create an environment that feels overly oppressive and stifling. It can strip the relationship of its natural balance and harmony. It may lead to resentment, fear, and a loss of mutual respect, ultimately extinguishing the vibrancy of the marriage. The key to a lively and fulfilling marriage lies in a balanced approach to power and submission. When power is exercised with love and consideration, it creates a dynamic where both partners feel valued and respected. Submission, when it stems from love rather than fear, fosters a deep sense of connection and mutual respect. This dynamic of balanced approach brings life to the marriage, as both individuals feel empowered and appreciated.

- **Intelligent behaviour** often resolves the conflict. Next, **experience** will help. **Literary knowledge** brings maturity to the couples.

Marriage is the pursuit of fulfillment in life. Marriage is seeking for the fulfillment which has not existed in life so far. But in practice, marriage destroys even the satisfaction that existed so far. Everyone is interested in calling themselves an ideal couple. The characteristic of marriage depicted in literature and films, is not in the life, is the experience.

Important basics of marriage

1. There is no outcome without effort.
2. Relationship is love, not power.
3. If there is no authority, there is a way for the birth of love.
4. He who would do anything, if possible, is not a man. He cannot be a husband. "Because it can be done, I will get it done" is not good. She cannot become a wife.
6. Harmony will arise by the one who says, 'I can't fight.'
7. Others' defects are a source of conflict.

8. There is no fragrance if the mind seeks another person. Loyalty is a lifeline in a married relationship.

9. Cleanliness means cleanliness of hands, cleanliness of mouth and cleanliness of mind.

10. An unclean person gets nothing clean.

11. Without labour, there is no income.

12. Without responsibility, there is no comfort.

13. Without patience, there is nothing.

14. **Family Establishment**: Endeavor, love, character, harmony, cleanliness, hard work, responsibility, patience are the basis of any establishment. The best establishment, which is family, cannot be formed without them.

15. Man going to the moon is a skill. Family is not created by skills. **The embryo of the family is character. Characters create the family. Skills will raise it**.

Enhancing Marital Stability Through Premarital Training in American Churches

American churches instituted a 15-day practice for marriage when many young people were generally getting divorced within 10 days or 20 days of marriage due to inexperience. People who had this training did not divorce all of sudden. After seeing this, the church made it a law that if you want to get married in the American church, you must have this training.

- Knowing the details will prevent the mistakes that happen due to ignorance.

- Training can be given to overcome deficiencies arising from lack of experience.

Some of the graduates who join the Taluk office as Clerks today become Deputy Collector when completing their service. The same graduate is given 1½ years of training and is made Deputy Collector early in IAS. A Deputy Collector retires as Secretary and Governor. The basis for all that is this 1½ year training. A Deputy Collector rules half of a district. Marriage is about ruling the family. We can get trained for obtaining satisfaction in married life. We must learn that we can train ourselves. Such training centres if they come up in many numbers, divorce will drop from 50% to 5%. As this is not available currently, we should try to train ourselves.

- Problems that arise in marriage are simple problems.

- Training solves all simple problems totally.

- Families possessed of **Education, Character, City life, Civilisation** have lesser family conflicts. This shows that conflict can be avoided through training.

- Few days of training can give a person **experience of what is gained in many generations** through education and character. It is common for all fields. Marriage is no exception.

Not everyone needs all the training. Whatever problem arises, training is required for that problem only. Marriage is a relationship. It is a close relationship. Relationship means love. If there is only love, there will be no conflict. Human nature thinks of power, when it sees love. If you consider power, love will disappear and relationships will break. Who dominates whom is decided on the first or second day of the marriage. Man is subtle. He will not leave even if there is atom space to dominate. This is human nature.

Certain most important rules that one should follow for the satisfaction of marriage are as follows.

- There should be no argument as to which family is superior.

- Pointing out the faults of others must be avoided.

- If the other person has goodness, you should appreciate it. We can express ourselves through words. Instead of expressing by words, truly if our heart appreciates, the other person will know.

- If the fault of the husband's family is found in someone else, it should not be condemned in front of the husband. The fact that wife has talked about the other person only, is not justifiable. The husband feels hurt if the wife thinks that her husband's family habits are poor. If it hurts like that, it will not heal afterwards. Habits in a wife's family, if found in someone, if the husband accepts and appreciates, it will help in the union of the wife's mind with him forever.

- It is better to explain to someone who does not know the details. It is not enough to not say bad things as much as to say good things. Get it out of your mind. If it is inside the mind, it will come out one day.

- We should not ask what to do about the intolerableness in the other person. Neither husband nor wife is a third person. It is not intolerable. We should see and accept that intolerableness is there for us to learn patience. We do this in a place of authority. We are forced to display patience at the workplace submitting to authority. We must do this consciously in a marital relationship too. If you bow to love as much as you bow to authority, love that doesn't exist will also secrete.

- We should not try to change the other. If we try, we can change habits. We should not try to change their character. It will lead to permanent division. Even if it is accepted forcibly today, the situation may change and it will pave the way for the parting of the couple. The character which does not want to be changed will create the way for parting in life.

- Any shortcoming can be tried and overcome to some extent. It should be done. Mental discontent cannot be changed. So from the beginning as much as possible, not allow grievances to arise in the mind.

- Acceptance of husband by the wife and wife by the husband should be done heart fully. If the mind does not accept the other, there will be no fragrance. Although not yet, it is necessary to try and ask the mind to accept it.

- In the chapter on Decision-making (Four quadrant formula) it is explained how to make decisions to get things done. Decisions lead to successful accomplishment when both the external and internal requirements are fully positive. If the outside is complete and the inside is not deficient, the act will be accomplished. If the husband follows this law with his wife in important matters in the family and also the wife follows the same law, there will be two results.

1. All things done, will succeed.

2. Harmony prevails between husband and wife. It changes the domestic atmosphere drastically. That family is ushered into PROSPERITY. The real truth is PROSPERITY SEEKS THAT FAMILY.

Unegoistic behaviour makes family life flower

To an unegoistic view, the infinite ocean of energy reveals. Man is buried in the ego. He does not know the wonders of the infinite. Man who marries is buried in his smallness, selfishness, egoism, petty past, superstitious beliefs.

Married life above the social context, in the psychological sense, is an unfettered vast freedom where one enjoys relating to the other in her freedom. One can understand only by their experience. Man working on facts positively in his married life will be happy.

Ego shed in family is eternal joy and endless happiness. Shedding ego inwardly will prompt the other to shed his ego partly. The force is conscious. The force in the family is from the relationship of the husband and wife.

Life is more sensitive than Man. Our attitudes are at once responded to by life. Man has to overcome his opinion. Life has no opinion or prejudice to overcome. Be good, generate goodwill. The spouse will respond. If not, life will make the other respond. Consider what is common to both. Don't go by your own standard. Insisting on one's preference is domination. Accepting another's preference is submission. Actually, neither is desirable as there will be later repercussions on the opposite side. Between vegetarian and non-vegetarian food, the former is common which is one accepting other's preference. The common factor in these things is both want to enjoy food. There must be many food items both equally enjoy. More than that, there are very many items of life which both richly enjoy. Make an exhaustive list of them and confine life to them. Enjoyment of one aspect very much fully neutralises not enjoying another aspect. The idea of rising to the expectation of the spouse in such occasions works wonders here. One intent on pleasing the other drowns the other complaints. Family Life will flower.

Causes for strain in married life

- Interference from other family members leading to conflicts.
- Emergence of new habits post-marriage causing adjustment issues.
- Avoidance of unavoidable situations instead of accepting and addressing them.
- Influence of parents creating problems and disrupting the couple's life.
- Violation of traditional practices such as keeping a married woman at her mother's home.
- Problems arising from status differences, poverty consciousness, and power dynamics.
- Lack of love, affection, and understanding leading to temperamental issues.
- Status differences causing difficulties and misunderstandings in the relationship.

- Power struggles and dominance issues within the marriage.
- Lack of loyalty and emotional connection leading to dissolution of the marriage.

Nurturing Harmony in Marriage: Key Principles for a Fulfilling Relationship

Avoid criticism: Avoid criticising each other and instead focus on appreciating each other's goodness.

Acceptance: Embrace each other's habits and backgrounds with understanding and appreciation. Avoid trying to change each other's character to prevent permanent division. Respect the uniqueness that each partner brings to the relationship.

Communication and Understanding: Cultivate open and honest communication to address conflicts and misunderstandings effectively. Seek to understand each other's perspectives and feelings.

Loyalty: Maintain cleanliness not only physically but also in thoughts and actions.

Patience and Compassion: Impatience does greater harm than anger. Greed is more harmful than both. Practice patience and compassion in dealing with each other's shortcomings and challenges. Approach difficulties with a mindset of growth and mutual support.

Intelligent behaviour and experience: Endeavor to resolve conflicts through intelligent behaviour and experience.

Unity and Intimacy: Strive for unity and intimacy rather than power dynamics in the relationship, focusing on building a strong emotional connection and bond. Nurture moments of closeness and togetherness. Cultivate love, harmony, responsibility in the relationship.

Respect and Generosity: Show respect and generosity towards your partner, appreciating their efforts and contributions to the relationship. Avoid criticism and instead offer words of encouragement and support.

Mutual efforts and understanding: Seek fulfillment and satisfaction through mutual efforts and understanding.

Decision-Making and Consecration: Make important decisions together, considering each other's opinions and feelings. Embrace the concept of consecration in your relationship, aligning your actions with shared values and goals.

- Don't complain.
- Don't react with negativity.
- Don't try to one up the other person.
- Don't try to impose your will.
- Compliment on small things.
- Try to raise the level of harmony in all interactions and other times too.
- Treat partner as you would an honored guest.

Evoking Positive Life Response (For Quick Digest)

(even following one of the below can evoke positive conditions from life for you)

1. Complaining aggravates the behaviour it seeks to cure. Instead of complaining, focus on solutions. Lose the ability to complain.
2. The less you react, the less cause and provocation you will have for reaction. React Less, Listen More.
3. Disengage yourself from every conflict as soon as possible. Walk away from arguments to cool down before productive discussion.
4. Give your partner the benefit of the doubt.
5. A touch of patience dissolves disharmonies. True patience comes from self-understanding.
6. Refrain from using cynical humor, teasing, and sarcasm under the guise of being humorous. Such remarks act like acid rain, harming the delicate beauty of a rainforest.

7. Always refrain from attributing ulterior motives to your partner, even if you believe you have valid reasons to do so.

8. To truly overcome a problem, develop the ability to forget it entirely. Release past grievances without leaving a trace, allowing for lasting resolution.

9. Whenever you are very sure you are right, consider your partner's perspective. You'll often find valuable truths within it that deserve recognition and respect.

10. Being right and having your way are the triumph of ego, which destroys relationships. Instead, practice generosity, consideration, love, and selflessness to nurture strong and healthy connections.

11. The more you try to improve yourself and the less you try to change your partner, the better your relationship will become.

12. Recognise and acknowledge your partner's feelings and perceptions without passing judgment or criticism.

13. Undivided personal attention fosters intense affection.

14. Assuming full responsibility for improving the relationship without expecting anything in return from your partner is the most effective way to encourage their complete cooperation.

15. Learn to cherish the differences between you and your partner.

16. No act is too small or insignificant to serve as a means for expressing affection.

17. Don't take anything for granted. Acknowledge and give credit to your partner, where it is due, even for the smallest happy occurrence.

18. Silent Will is more effective than the spoken word. When you intensely want something from your partner, will for it silently rather than asking in words.

19. Listen to your partner's silences. Respond with understanding, acceptance and affection. Misunderstanding if pursued in the right spirit can reveal much that might have never come out, which can strengthen the relationship, or at least create a better one for the future.

It is another form of the journey from Ignorance to Knowledge, so key for evolution.

20. Gratitude Attracts More. Gratitude is a spiritual emotion that brings more of what we feel grateful for.

Taking up these methods will cause life to respond positively for both parties!

The Value of Inner Work: "Beyond Appearances: Self-Transformation is Never Wasted Effort"

A husband becomes angry, and the wife wisely avoids such situations. Conversely, when the wife is impatient, the husband avoids those scenarios, which is beneficial. However, understanding the reason behind his anger can reduce its intensity. Instead, if you know why he is angry, your knowledge will lessen the force of his anger. Often it may be in your power to remove the cause of his anger. Thus you come to know the physical cause. It helps physically. You may be able to know the psychological cause. In case you are able to remove it, the results will be greater. The greater positive results will raise the level of atmosphere at home. Further if you can know the corresponding words, thoughts, feelings in you that trigger his anger, it acts as a deeper force when you remove the negatives in you by inner work. Such an effort when pursued will lead to transformation. Impatience in the wife is caused by several outer or inner occasions.

There will be corresponding points outer or inner in the husband. Effort to remove anything negative in the inner is sincerity. Sincerity is an unfailing power. Such efforts are parallel to raising one's salary from Rs.1,00,000 to Rs.10,00,000. Of course, such effort, also, often raises the salary like this as a by-product. Marriage provides a family, which is a source of health, joy, and support. Turning the family into a source of higher joy ensures its enduring positivity. Perennial rivers do not dry. Just like perennial rivers, such a family will not dry up but will flourish beyond measure.

There is no waste in Nature. What takes most people fifty or a hundred years to achieve, some can accomplish in just five or ten years. To onlookers, their activities might seem wasteful, but for these achievers, extraordinary gains are evident, and they overlook the apparent waste. Nature attempts infinite works simultaneously achievable in centuries or millennia and completes it in some years or decades. To man, this process may appear as a massive waste. However, in Nature, even the apparent waste in an achiever's life does not truly exist.

Every particle of energy achieves a thousand-fold as the entire work is integrated. Every effort and particle of energy spent for one's transformation by doing inner work seeing the corresponding point in the spouse will strengthen their relationship, lift both of them in the evolutionary ladder as well as raising the family atmosphere bringing in quantum prosperity. There is no waste in our inner work.

Problems are coming to solve us

Do everything inside you, for the world to respond. Don't expect. Go inside, work on correspondences. The rule is known. Implement it. Nothing equals inner work.

Take it as work, not a triumph. Please know every work will be done perfectly. There is no problem. Problem is in our view, not in itself. We think in terms of solving problems. ***Problems will solve themselves. Problems are capable of solving us.*** We do not know that. Problems are coming to solve our inner deficiencies. Problems aid our evolution.

At home, man has a wife. He can love her, if she does not. If she loves him there will be no problem in his world. If he loves her, he cannot have any problem. Even on the strength of his own love, her problems will be solved.

Problems are a way of life that seeks low intensity. Seeking intensity at a higher level, they will disappear. Our own problems are opportunities to others. Our opportunities are higher opportunities to others. Individuals have intensities, intense sensitivity. Why touch it, leave it to itself. Reaching another's intense sensitivity, you share it. It is a simple rule of self-preservation. ***Life is calm, good unless you disturb others or allow others to disturb you.***

Never attribute ulterior motives to your partner, even when you feel justified.

Whenever you are very sure you are right, take your partner's point of view. You will always discover a truth in it that should be honored.

Chastity: Goodwill = Goodness+ Will

Man or woman in life loves to rise. Chastity in this restricted domestic sense is a powerful instrument for one's development. The components of chastity are many.

The two that stand out are WILL and its GOODNESS – GOODWILL. The main strand of this is pure original GOODWILL to the spouse. Absence of ill-will is not goodwill. Selfish goodwill is greed, and will not have that power. **To generate GOODWILL for another is not in human power**, except for good souls born with it. It will not get generated easily. It must be pure of mercenary motives. Further, it must reach an intensity that is capable of crossing the human limit and passing into the divine arena. Should a couple develop such original, pure, intense goodwill for each other, whatever they attempt will be easily accomplished. In families that rapidly rise, we see this type of goodwill present, after a fashion, during the period of that growth.

 Acting in faith in the partner's goodness which is in abundance, a field of Patience will raise marriage into Romance.

Three dimensions of a person

Once a person meets with an initial success, the person must work on all their traits consciously. Life will brighten as a light is turned on in a dark room. A person has three dimensions, ***individual, universal, transcendent.*** Man is a person, he is the head of the family and he is divine.

- As a person he can keep his wife happy and contented.
- As a head of the family he can make her life abundant and inwardly rich.
- As divine, he can persuade her to be his spiritual complement.

The first needs social discipline.

The second demands psychological self-discipline.

The last is exacting, as he has to follow yogic rules in domestic life.

Psychological self-discipline is intense goodwill irrespective of what the other is. Yogic formula is to treat the other as one's inner complement meaning whatever she does, he must see, originates in his subconscious.

The one strategy of knowing the other man's point of view practiced by even one partner, will bring about a sea change. Both adhering to it, the family will change out of recognition. Happiness will become joy. Joy will become delight.

A harmonious marriage is built on a foundation of love, respect, and understanding. By following these key principles of acceptance, communication, patience, unity, and respect, couples can nurture a strong and fulfilling relationship that withstands the test of time. Prioritising harmony and unity in married life, fostering a deep and meaningful connection brings joy and fulfillment to both partners. By doing the Inner work and understanding the subtle-truths of life, one will be in position not only to rapidly self-transform oneself but also act as a powerful instrument in aiding evolution of the spouse, their children and all those who are associated with this ALL POWERFUL spirited individual.

****END OF SIX PARTS ****

Epilogue

A. *IGNORANCE, KNOWLEDGE, EVOLUTIONARY AIM*

As we look around, how many of us are satisfied with what we see? Each one of us experiences the increasing pressure for change. It is the individual that is the source of creativity that enables social evolution to happen; and it is the level of consciousness of the individuals in a society that makes up the level of consciousness of that society. Social change begins with individual change.

And what we change within will also vibrate out and change the corresponding aspect(s) in the world.

Existence is a horizontal movement.
Evolution is a vertical movement.

— At the lowest point, existence moves in conflicting
dualities opposing each other.
— At the highest point, existence moves from stage to
stage without confronting the conflicts.
— As the movement at the highest point of existence is
saturated, it begins to move vertically.
— As the vertical movement begins, the individual life
begins to secure the full support of wider life. At this point it turns into luck because the wider life is full of material plenty.

We as Individuals in evolution emerging from Inconscient and ascending to Superconscient have to continuously upgrade ourselves from dumb conception of delight to luminous consummation of delight.

The entire evolutionary journey is all about the increase of consciousness and experience of delight in the Existence.

This World Existence is a masked form of Satchitananda.

Everything in the universe is seeking for the self-delight which is hidden in Existence. The fundamental impulse of our life is to seek delight. An individual is a product of the universe. We are the ancestors who can change everything for our descendants.

As humans, filled with golden divine light, we can choose to mutate and emerge as a new Supramental Species. The power of human choice can go to that extent. God gives the option. Man makes his choice.

- Destiny is a choice.
- God gives total Freedom.
- Man exercises the choice in Freedom.
- The choice exercised in his favour is destiny.
- The choice exercised as God intends is evolution.
- **Luck is Man accepting the choice of his evolution.**

The individual must recover its right relation and harmony with the totalities of which it forms a part. Self-knowledge is to discover the universal in the individual and the spiritual in the physical. Strength issues from universality.

We each represent an impossibility that can become a possibility. This is why we are here, what our evolving Soul yearns to more fully comprehend through our progress.

And there also may be a Universal Soul that too is evolving, which through our development we partake in. In that way, we play an integral part in a universal process of Becoming, which itself is an instrument of a Transcendent Will that seeks manifestation of its spiritual qualities in the universe.

Sri Aurobindo says the universe evolves through the evolution of the psychic soul in Man, thereby fulfilling the Divine Intent.

During the first phase of evolution, all progress is by conflict between forms. Contact of form with form releases force. Contact of force with force releases consciousness. Pain has secret widening power. Pain is an intense Delight. Pain has immensity and not infinity. There is no pain which has no secret widening power.

Our suffering is due to our lack of wisdom of subtle laws of life. An action becomes an adventure when there is opposition. Ultimately what we receive from life is only the knowledge irrespective of whatever we may seek during our life.

Our Surface mind is deeper Eternal Self adventuring in Time. The Eternal Self in us carries out its adventure in the playground of our surface mind in Time. The surface mind which faces the outer challenges of our life is an extension of deeper Eternal Self in us.

Psychological learning is integral learning. It brings us psychological evolution. In the measure we effect psychological evolution in us, in that measure we can see evolution in our outer life.

1. If Personality changes into Impersonality,
   Individuality turns into Universality.
2. Ignorance is knowledge in the making.
   Pain is a delight in the making.

3. Ignorance is an intense form of self-lost knowledge.

    Pain is an intense form of self -lost delight.

4. Ignorance is the seeking of knowledge.

    Pain is the seeking delight.

5. Ignorance is hidden knowledge.

    Pain is hidden delight.

6. The knowledge obtained after ignorance is richer than the original pure knowledge which existed prior Creation.

The delight obtained after pain is richer delight than the original pure delight or bliss which existed prior creation.

The Supreme Reality, Absolute Divine which existed before Creation self -lost, self- hidden itself through Involution and emerges in Evolution in MANY forms, as many species experience RICHER knowledge and delight of Existence than it experienced when it was ALONE and as ONE. The Supreme Reality by self-conception, self- limitation, self -absorption has become this Creation. As Evolution starts from the other side of Superconscient, that is from Inconscient, our evolutionary experiences are marked with Ignorance, Suffering, Evil, Falsehood, and miseries. But as more progress and knowledge comes in, the evolution in ignorance and suffering will turn into evolution in knowledge and delight. Thus the aim of Creation is to give richer experience to the Absolute Supreme Reality, SatChitAnanda.

Involution Vs. Evolution

INVOLUTION (The process of Creation- Descent from Superconscient to Inconscient) reverses into EVOLUTION (The process of Manifestation, Ascent from Inconscient to Superconscient).

When ignorance gradually evolves into knowledge, it discovers the Unity behind the division and transforms itself from divided ignorance to united knowledge.

1. Inconscience seeks ignorance.

2. Ignorance seeks knowledge.

3. Knowledge seeks realisation.

4. This realisation in our BEING is partial.(Inner realisation in depths)

5. It has to mature into realisation in our BECOMING.(Outer realisation in our surface consciousness).

6. Further it has to mature into realisation of the BEING of the BECOMING which is total and integral.

This is the PROCESS. Thus the evolution and transformation are graded.

Difference between Moksha and Transformation

Moksha gives liberation for the soul. It is the escape of the soul back to its origin, shunning life and existence. Daring soul seeks not moksha but transformation. It is embracing life and transforming it into a divine life by inner transformation. *The distance between moksha and transformation is some thousand years.*

Spirit is the substance of which the entire universe is made.

Religious worship is following the other's awakening. **Religion is following the awakened spirit of the other. Spirituality is awakening to one's inner spirit.** Spiritual illumination is awakening within oneself. It is awakening to the Spirit within oneself.

The aim of evolutionary nature is heightening of our consciousness so that we manifest and become manifold power of the Spirit. Spirit, which is known to be immutable, is mutable, says Sri Aurobindo. It evolves through many human births. Hence, the necessity of rebirth.

Man is not the end. The next species of the supramental being will be on earth by man's rising to the Supramental planc and the Supermind descending on earth. The advent of Sri Aurobindo on the spiritual horizon of the world is a new age. It is the age of the Supermind. Essentially it is the beginning of the recognition that the age of mind is over and the future is for the Supermind. It is seen as, *Turning away from moksha towards transformation.*

- One part of the being, the Spirit, leaving man for its origin, is moksha.
- All parts of the being allowing their spiritual element to surface for transformation is the thing called for currently.

Stages of Evolution

There are various stages from identification with our lower nature to self-awareness, self-control to spiritual freedom. Evolution of consciousness moves from vital animality to mental morality to spiritual knowledge of the Supreme Will. Each has a place in the evolutionary progression. Unconsciousness of our defects to self-justification of them to self-condemnation and regret are stages in our progress to the joy of spiritual detachment and freedom from ignorant lower nature. Each stage has its rightful role in our progress from bondage to nature to true free will. Conversion of pain into ananda can best be understood by seeing that our psychological sorrows often get converted into joy later on when we see the eventual outcome of something we deeply regret. The same principle applies at the physical level when we outgrow the reaction of pain to experience the ananda behind every happening.

Consciousness –Key for Quantum Evolution

Recent discoveries in quantum physics indicate that nothing fundamentally exists in the universe; that the underlying quantum particles have no material reality and exist only as mathematical potentials. Then what binds the universe; what is the truth behind these quantum particles? It is Consciousness. The Conscious-Force of the Infinite Divine is actually what we recognise as quantum particles that is the basis of all existence. That would make everything in the universe Divine in essence. *The real secret of quantum evolution is in the growth of consciousness which happens by our inner work.*

Evolution-Beyond Vedanta

Vedanta is the essence of Hinduism, as experienced by the Rishis who saw into the nature of Reality, including its spiritual Source. Sri Aurobindo took it much further into the modern age. He explained in great detail the involutionary process from spirit to matter culminating in the universe, as well as the evolution from matter to spirit that can culminate in a divine life on earth. Between these two processes, Supermind created space-time, subject-object, the spiritual values of creation, etc. and it now serves as the Spiritual Force we can evoke to bring about sudden good fortune in our lives and the spiritual transformation of life on earth.

Real Adventure is within

We can dedicate ourselves to a life of conscious evolution, with the purpose of evolving our nature to our highest possibility and potential. It would be a journey from our current status to our ultimate human and spiritual potential.

If we are interested in such an undertaking, how would we begin? The first major step of conscious evolution is to make the effort to come out of ego – which is the main bar to discovering our higher nature.

We do that by moving our Centre of consciousness away from the surface of life and into the depths within. There we discover a stillness and silence that engenders a level of awareness and mindfulness of the flow of life, of the truths unfolding, and the needs and concerns of those around us. As we move away from the surface bubbling, the visual and auditory stimuli of the senses that pours in through our senses, we discover a deeper poise within, a stillness that aligns us more tightly with the rest of the world. As a result, our sense of separateness and, hence, our self-centeredness and ego begin to dissolve.

The future evolution of man lies in the inner work. The real adventure is within.

Inner Guide and Self within

There is no bottom to the depths within, as there is no limit to how we can connect to, align with, and meld with the world around us. Behind the calm and silence we experience, there is a deeper Subliminal being that sends up its positive influences to the surface. Anyone who has ever experienced that sudden thought that warns us of what action to avoid, or what course to take in a cross-roads moment, has known the influence of that **Inner Guide**.

Deeper still we discover our **True Selves**, our personal evolving Soul within. There we discover our highest nature and being; that which illuminates our deepest purpose in life; that which connects us to the transcendent spirit; that which binds us to all around us, and to the unfoldings of life. Love, harmony, oneness, and bliss issue from there.

As we continually move to the deeper parts of our being – from silence and stillness to the Inner Guidance of the subliminal to our Evolving Souls within – our separative ego consciousness gives way, and our true nature blossoms. At that point we will have made the decisive change that takes us from our old nature to a new super-nature. At that point, we are well on our way of personal progress and our own **conscious evolution**.

Evolutionary roots of Evil in Ignorance

Falsehood and evil exist for the same reason that Ignorance exists—because the one infinite consciousness has manifested itself as universe through a process of involution. This process of involution and creation consists of 3 steps, namely, self-conception, self-limitation and self-absorption.

The infinite consciousness consciously limits and loses itself in self-absorption within the forms which it creates out of itself, so that it may have the *joy of self-discovery in a progressive evolutionary unfolding* of its infinity in the terms of a finite universe. It is for this reason that the infinite consciousness chooses this apparently imperfect method for manifestation, i.e. evolution through Ignorance.

B. BRAIN, MIND, CONSCIOUSNESS

Brain Vs. Mind

Analogy of a television set clearly explains the difference between mind and brain. A primitive man seeing a TV for the first time would naturally conclude that the people he sees on the screen are somehow contained inside the set. What else could he possibly conclude? To consider an alternative viewpoint, he has to first concede that the voices and images of real people can be converted into invisible waves, transmitted over long distances and rematerialised at the other end, notions that are utterly preposterous.

If a television set can receive and translate electromagnetic waves into sound and picture, why can't the human brain act in similar fashion? Is it any more realistic to believe that atoms and molecules self-constitute themselves into Shakespeare's love sonnets and Leonardo da Vinci's Mona Lisa?

Brain is like a TV. The brain is an instrument, not the creator of thought. Mind is anterior to the instrument. Brain is merely an instrument of Mind. Brain is the physical seat of mind. Mind has developed the brain and nerves in the course of its development of the body.

The mind's function is to divide. By dividing it is able to concentrate on the part, not on the whole.

The mechanic will remember the defect of the car, not the particular car itself. Mind de-pieces things for analysis and comprehension. It can only be understood through parts. To understand the whole, we have to transcend beyond mind and go to **consciousness**. What cannot be understood by mind, can be understood by consciousness. Consciousness replaces thoughts.

If we know and remember the whole and keep within the rules of the whole, we will be successful in our actions, in the parts. The railways are the whole. If we want to get into the train from beside the track, it will not work. Even if we are the Minister of the Railways, it will not work. We have to get on the train from the platform. It means we have to ***respect the whole and function within the rules of the whole, stay in tune with the whole***. When we lose contact with the whole, our parts become mismatch to the whole. It is not energy, skill, opinion, attitude or character, either singly or in combination, that ultimately determines the results of action. It is consciousness. As is the consciousness, so is the result.

- Consciousness is the key.
- In discovering the hidden consciousness, lies the secret.
- Discovery yields delight.
- Self-discovery offers the maximum Delight. God seeks it.
- God created the Universe in pursuit of that Delight.
- He became the finite, Inconscient Universe so that He might evolve back to His original status, thus enjoying Delight in the process.
- His becoming the inert universe involves the inversion of Being into Inconscient Matter, Infinite into Finite, Eternity into Time.
- He has created no evil or pain, but only delight.
- The inversion occurs at all points of Satchidananda as Light into Darkness. Knowledge into Ignorance, Ananda into Pain, Truth into Falsehood.
- In the process of the above inversion, Mind gets created.
- Mind is a dividing Instrument. That division creates the separative ego. The ego suffers pain, evil, etc. There is no evil or pain in creation.
- Emerging out of the ego is the part of Man, the most enlightened member of evolution.

- Evil is thus answered.

- Things that enter man unconsciously can only leave him when he is conscious of them.

- What comes to someone from the outside without his knowledge cannot leave him without his knowledge.

- The Universe is a lock and the individual is the key.

- Transformation is a silent resolution and movement.

- More we grow in our inner consciousness, the more we see the logic of the unforeseen, and the more we understand the logic of the Infinite.

Mind is an instrument for consciousness to know things in particular. But when things are to be known in general, mind has to transcend itself and attain the consciousness behind.

Mind gives the knowledge of the APPEARANCE of the life experiences. Consciousness gives the knowledge of the ESSENCE of life experiences.

Mind has to rise higher and expand in CONSCIOUSNESS to attain the ESSENCE of the knowledge behind the APPEARANCE of the knowledge.

No higher knowledge can come to the mind which has not risen itself higher and expanded. Mind is not a faculty of knowledge. It is a faculty of seeking for knowledge. Mind keeps certain coins of truth in the bank of memory.

In fact, the mind itself is an aspect of consciousness. When the imaginary wall is broken by the experiences and knowledge and when the mind is transcended and consciousness is realised.

Whatever we have seen so far as problems and difficulties will be seen as opportunities for our progress and evolution.

Consciousness comes to us as relationships. Relationships come to us as experiences. Experiences come to us for our evolution.

In consciousness our problems dissolve and disappear.

In proportion we raise from limitations of our mind, in the same proportion the unlimited problems become gradually limited thereupon dissolving and disappearing.

Rather than the expansion of mind, the consciousness expansion is more important.

Progress has to happen in consciousness. Progress of the mind can be called horizontal progress and the progress of the consciousness which is real progress is vertical progress.

Knowing the object through senses gives us one level of experience. When the same object is seen through the mind we acquire the capacity to operate the object and derive the benefit by functioning of the object. But if the same object when seen through the consciousness, the essence of the object comes to us.

It is always greater to know a thing through consciousness rather than through mind as consciousness is greater than mind. When a problem comes to us, we deal with it through our mind, sink in it and suffer. When the same problem is seen through our consciousness, we acquire the capacity to know the cause of the problem and knowledge for removal of it.

When **mind observes** life outer problems, such **problems of our life** are solved by mind. Likewise when our **consciousness observes** our problems in our mind, the **problems of our mind** is solved.

The problem created by an instrument, a part cannot be solved by the same instrument. For solving the problem, higher instruments are required.

When the mind sees the problem it brings its own limitations in the problems.

Unless the mind becomes aware of the vast consciousness behind it, no realisation can come. If mind stops, consciousness acts.

It is said that all solutions are contained in problems. All problems are contained in our inner selves.

When difficult situations or problems come to us, it is the right moment to rise and expand in our consciousness instead of shrinking within ourselves. Such problems are the opportunities for our growth.

The law of the world is whatever we search for we get, whatever we don't search for we don't get. Rising in our inner, we get the thing without searching for it. That is to get the thing by not searching we have to rise in our inner. Such inner change brings great Life Response.

This is an operation of higher law and higher principle.

The Central Message of Life Response:

Changes in consciousness instantly attract good fortune; indicating that the inner is the true determinant of the outer.

C. *FEW OUTER EVIDENCES OF INNER WORK*

Our shifting from outer to the inner, expanding in our inner, brings great LIFE RESPONSE.

Some outer indications of inner expansion.

1. Even a casual utterance made by someone resonates deeply in you to bring greater realisation.
2. Causeless joy arises within you.
3. Thinking about others, instead of fear, jealousy, greed, positive emotions like love, happiness, joy, gratitude arises within.
4. Even an impossible task will seem possible and become effortless for you to do.

5. Your mind loses its rigidity and become flexible.

6. Your mind changes in accordance with the situations and things instead of your mind struggling to change the situations and things.

7. Mental and emotional atmosphere remain positive.

8. The things which others see negatively, will be seen positively by you.

9. You start seeing the opportunities behind the apparent negatives.

10. Instead of seeing opportunities life experiences as problems, you start seeing problems as opportunities and life experiences.

11. Faith in the Spirit and Divine increases.

12. Aspiration for learning, always flame within you regardless of age.

13. The flame of aspiration to attain wisdom always exists.

14. You lose your capacity to get angry.

15. Ego blunts.

16. Impulsion, urges, and reaction will be in self-control.

17. You recognise peace, silence dwelling within.

18. You become bigger than the situation.

19. Resilience, confidence, courage increases.

20. Body, heart, mind surrender to the Spirit within.

21. Even if there is pain or trouble, it does not last long.

22. In short, you will be able to connect to the inner guide and spirit within and tap into an inner reservoir of unlimited potential for manifestation and accomplishment for living a fulfilled and soulful life.

"Self- experience and self-expression is sought by the soul in the birth"

– Sri Aurobindo

When you accept your higher conscious being and allow it to become part of your personality, part of your state of consciousness, it has the ability to move the outer events on its own. Your inner state, inner mental and emotional atmosphere is the DETERMINANT of everything.

D. *BENEFITS OF A NEW WAY OF LIVING DUE TO INNER WORK*

1. You embrace higher values in life.
2. Your capacity to Attain-Retain-Sustain resourceful state increases.
3. You understand the subtle laws of Life.
4. You hear the silent voice of Life.
5. You will be in silent communion with Life and Universe.
6. You will see Life and Universe is working for you to fulfill your being.
7. Your speed of accomplishment in life increases.
8. Your perception of yourself, people, and things changes radically.
9. By understanding that people on Earth are in different timelines of evolution, jealousy and comparison goes out, compassion and love comes in.
10. Your relationship with others becomes more understanding and harmonious.
11. Your self-giving, humility increases.
12. Whatever accomplished so far by you putting maximum efforts, reaping minimum results will reverse the formula as minimum efforts, maximum results.
13. Spirit replaces ego. Ego which was the axis around which your life was revolving will turn around to Spirit becoming the axis and centre of you and your life.
14. Consciousness gradually replaces thoughts.
15. You start seeing the significance behind each insignificant life event.
16. You will become a life response reader.

17. Good fortune sails to you without your effort.

18. Luck continually comes your way.

19. You move life from within.

20. Your orientation and poise shifts to inner.

21. Your mindfulness and witness consciousness increases.

22. Your harmony with life increases.

23. Your feeling of a deep sense of oneness with others increases.

24. You sense a deeper purpose in life.

25. Your inner sense of knowingness increases.

26. You are in tune with the events of life.

27. You are consistently selfless and self-giving.

28. You are unceasingly selfless and giving.

29. Life within you is calm, peaceful and equal.

30. All your wishes come true and quickly.

31. Your receptivity and openness to the Spirit increases.

32. Life conditions come under your control.

33. You increasingly see the Spirit's Force working on your behalf.

34. The infinite surfaces in the current finite.

35. In the present, the future takes shape.

36. Time abridges. Your capacity to accomplish increases.

37. You feel great joy in living.

38. You feel a spiritual presence above and within.

39. You are constantly growing and changing.

40. You are a pioneer of a new way of life.

41. Helps in anchoring your consciousness at a deeper level, rather than merely skimming the surface of existence.

42. Helps in gaining more clarity and insight.

43. Helps you to be in touch with the multiplicity of truths unfolding around you.

44. Helps you to understand the science of life.

45. Helps you to understand the significance of your life's movements and moments.

46. Helps you to understand the way the life responds, reason behind life response, to consciously evoke a positive life response.

47. Helps you to be in the inner based poise of self awareness and self consciousness.

48. Helps you to get connected to your inner spirit which is the primary lever, a means of your evolutionary change and transform yourself.

49. By connecting to your inner self you perceive your ultimate purpose in life and open to the vast array of insights, opportunities and feel more energetic and alive.

50. Helps in discovering your higher nature, reverse your consciousness, uplift your being and make transformational change.

51. Capacities dramatically get enhanced.

52. Feeling abiding joy in being alive.

53. Regeneration of the consciousness that was lost due to your self-absorption in the surface and outward consciousness and self-limitation.

54. Shed the limits of your own human makeup and prison.

55. Opens the possibility of a new spirit-based life and existence.

56. Gain a new inner view of yourself and of life.

57. Gain understanding of why there is difficulty and pain in life and the way out.

58. Aids to elevate your life so that you can realise your hopes, dreams and shift from leading a dissatisfied life to lead a satisfied life by fulfilling your intense longings and deeper aspirations.

59. Help you to shed limited perceptions and beliefs.

60. Help to evoke the powers of the Spirit and accomplish great results in the shortest period of time with least effort.

61. Helps you to navigate to your inner core of being and your inner sanctuary of presence and act from the inner poise within.

62. You will be navigated to new frontiers in your inner space and gain new insight about the makeup and purpose of life and existence.

63. Helps you to station above in your higher consciousness.

64. Helps you to garner your inner truth and inner reality.

65. Helps you to get yourself washed over by higher consciousness.

66. Helps you to navigate gradually to your deepest depths within, the wellspring of the spirit within.

67. Helps you to witness a titanic flow of your inner potentials seeking to manifest in your outer life.

68. Your inner antenna will be alive to know and understand things from a deep inner sense of knowingness and to take decisions and actions.

69. Helps you to become dynamic, creative, bold, bright and brilliant, illumined expressions and best version of yourself.

70. You experience a new dawn in your life.

71. Most of the minor problems vanish.

72. Atmosphere at home and workplace will become positive.

73. For unsolved major problems some solutions appear on horizon.

74. You feel spirit as your constant companion.

75. You dare to be adventurous.

76. You come out of your comfort zone.

77. You constantly challenge yourself to excel.

78. You learn the art of overcoming karma by reversal of consciousness.

79. You feel the inner fullness and feel the spiritual richness.

80. New opportunities sail towards you from the atmosphere in life.

81. You find yourself in a new environment which will offer you new opportunities.

82. Spirit will surface and your energies will continue to be on rise.

83. You will be filled with inner richness, fullness, ever present joy.

84. Your capacity to remain cheerful increases irrespective of outer conditions and events.

85. You start connecting the dots of currently perceived bewildering life.

86. You start taking a quantum leap towards Prosperity consciousness.

87. Your understanding of yourself, others and life heightens, deepens, widens.

88. _Unconscious Evolution,_ evolution in _Ignorance And Pain_ changes to _Conscious Evolution_ and evolution in _Knowledge, Joy And Harmony_.

89. Your Life Intelligence increases.

90. Your Emotional intelligence increases.

91. Your Mental intelligence increases.

92. Your Spiritual intelligence increases.

93. You celebrate life.

94. You move TOWARDS the FUTURE and move AWAY from the PAST and become balanced and whole.

95. Your inner dialogue and quality of your self-talk changes.

96. You drop the PERCEPTUAL FILTERS and become a CREATIVE DIRECTOR of your own theatre of life.

97. You become greater than the cause and the effect.

98. You become bigger than the situation instead of allowing the situation to become bigger than you.

99. You break into the Infinite within.

100. By intensifying inner work and transformation, you not only rise in your consciousness, you simply rise out of human consciousness and acquire a new way of being and living based on Spirit. It will be a Divine Life.

You become the ARCHITECT of your life.

> *"O Force-compelled, Fate-driven earth-born race,*
> *O petty adventurers in an infinite world*
> *And prisoners of a dwarf humanity,*
> *How long will you tread the circling tracks of mind*
> *Around your little self and petty things?*
> *But not for a changeless littleness were you meant,*
> *Not for vain repetition were you built,*
> *Almighty powers are shut in Nature's cells.*
> *A greater destiny awaits you in your front,*
> *The life you lead conceals the light you are."*
>
> —Savitri, Sri Aurobindo

> *"I saw them cross the twilight of an age,*
> *The sun-eyed children of a marvellous dawn*
> *The massive barrier-breakers of the world*
> *The architects of immortality*
> *Bodies made beautiful by the Spirit's light,*
> *Carrying the magic word, the mystic fire,*
> *Carrying the Dionysian cup of joy,*
> *Approaching eyes of a diviner man,*
> *Lips chanting an unknown anthem of the soul,*
> *Feet echoing in the corridors of Time.*
> *High priests of wisdom, sweetness, might and bliss,*
> *Discoverers of beauty's sunlit ways*
> *And swimmers of Love's laughing fiery floods*
> *And dancers within rapture's golden doors,*
> *Their tread one day shall change the suffering earth*
> *And justify the light on Nature's face.*

Although Fate lingers in the high Beyond

And the work seems vain on which our heart's force was spent,

All shall be done for which our pain was borne.

Even as of old man came behind the beast

This high divine successor surely shall come

Behind man's inefficient mortal pace,

Behind his vain labour, sweat and blood and tears:

He shall know what mortal mind barely durst think,

He shall do what the heart of the mortal could not dare.

Inheritor of the toil of human time,

He shall take on him the burden of the gods;

All heavenly light shall visit the earth's thoughts,

The might of heaven shall fortify earthly hearts;

Earth's deeds shall touch the superhuman's height,

Earth's seeing widen into the infinite.

—Savitri, Sri Aurobindo

References

1. https://www.karmayogi.net

2. https://www.motherservice.org

3. The Book -The Spiritual Individual in quest of the living organisation - Codec for the Infinite Game- Garry Jacobs

4. Life Response in Work- Roy Posner

5. A Life Response Reader- Roy Posner

6. A New Way of Living- Roy Posner

7. The Vital Difference -Unleashing the Powers of Sustained Corporate Success - Frederick Harmon, Garry Jacobs

8. The Vital Corporation- How American Businesses Large and Small Double Profits in Two Years or less -Garry Jacobs, Robert Macfarlane

9. Take charge of your life- Dr. Richard Bandler

10. Introducing NLP- Psychological Skills for Understanding and Influencing People -Joseph O'connor & John Seymour

Note to the readers

Readers who are interested to know more about the subject can find ample resources in the following websites:

1. https://www.karmayogi.net/

2. https://www.motherservice.org/

3. http://royposner.weebly.com/all-books.html

About the Author

N.M. Nageswari, author, personal mentor, spiritual guide, and life coach backed by her corporate working experience and her dedicated exploration of Inner work, human evolution, life response and life transformation for over 30 years brings you the 100 secret life-truths to empower your journey.

As an ICF Certified Innermost Shift Coach and Dr. Richard Bandler's Licensed NLP Practitioner, she offers a unique blend of skills to guide individuals on their transformative journeys and navigate the path to inner awakening.

Her passion extending beyond life-exploration and coaching, blossomed into the two-volume masterpiece, "Prayers of the Body for Divine Life: Pathways to Supramental Species" (February 2023). Available on Amazon (paperback/Kindle), Volume 1 offers 5555 prayers, while Volume 2 provides 6666 prayers – a powerful resource for your spiritual evolution. This second series of her book "Making Life Respond by Inner Work" –Unlocking 100 Secret Life-Truths released in 3 volumes, helps sincere seekers to bring the change in their inner being, to understand the science of life, life's behaviour and to master the art of moving life from within.

Embrace your inner transformation. Explore her work and Shine your Inner Light.

Connect with her on social media:

Mail:- motherdivine12@gmail.com

https://instagram.com/Naag6666

https://facebook.com/Naag333

https://linkedin.com/in/naag333

https://www.youtube.com/@nageswari2296

https://linktr.ee/naag333

www.ingramcontent.com/pod-product-compliance
Lightning Source LLC
Chambersburg PA
CBHW040726120726
48010CB00001B/23